Readings in Literary Criticism IV
CRITICS ON MARLOWE

CRITICS ON MARLOWE

Readings in Literary Criticism
Edited by Judith O'Neill

University of Miami Press
Coral Gables, Florida

PR
2674
C5   R 73   926
1970

ACKNOWLEDGMENT

M. C. Bradbrook: from *Themes and Conventions of Elizabethan Tragedy*, 1935. Cambridge University Press. Reprinted by permission of the publisher.

C. F. Tucker Brooke: from *Essays on Shakespeare and Other Elizabethans*. Copyright 1948 by Yale University Press. Reprinted by permission of the publishers.

C. F. Tucker Brooke: from *The Life of Marlowe and The Tragedy of Dido, Queen of Carthage*, ed. by C. F. Tucker Brooke. Copyright 1930 by Associated Book Publishers Ltd. (Methuen). Reprinted by permission of Gordian Press, New York.

Nicholas Brooke: from *The Cambridge Journal*, vol. V., no. II, 1952. Copyright 1952 by Nicholas Brooke. Reprinted by permission of Bowes & Bowes (Publishers) Ltd., London.

John Russell Brown: from 'Marlowe and the Actors', first published in *Tulane Drama Review*, vol. 8, no. 4, Summer 1964. Copyright © 1964 by *The Drama Review*. Reprinted by permission of the author and *The Drama Review*.

T. S. Eliot: from 'Christopher Marlowe' in *Selected Essays, New Edition*, by T. S. Eliot. Copyright 1932, 1936, 1950 by Harcourt, Brace & World, Inc.; copyright 1960, 1964 by T. S. Eliot. Reprinted by permission of the publishers.

U. M. Ellis-Fermor: from *Christopher Marlowe*, 1927. Methuen & Co. Ltd., London. Reprinted by permission of Archon Books, Hamden, Conn.

William Empson: from 'Two Proper Crimes', *The Nation*, vol. CLXIII, Oct. 19, 1946. Reprinted by permission of *The Nation*.

Helen Gardner: from *Modern Language Review*, vol. XXXVII, 1942. Copyright 1942 by Modern Humanities Research Association. Reprinted by permission of the author and Modern Humanities Research Association.

J. Leslie Hotson: from *The Death of Christopher Marlowe*, 1925. Harvard University Press, Cambridge, and The Nonesuch Press, London. Reprinted by permission of the publishers.

Leo Kirschbaum: from *The Review of English Studies*, vol. XIX, no. 75, 1943. Copyright 1943 by The Clarendon Press. Reprinted by permission of The Clarendon Press.

G. Wilson Knight: from *The Golden Labyrinth: A Study of British Drama*. Copyright © 1962 by G. Wilson Knight. Reprinted by permission of W. W. Norton & Co., Inc.

Clifford Leech: from *The Critical Quarterly*, vol. I, no. 3, 1959. Copyright © 1959 by Clifford Leech. Reprinted by permission of the author and *The Critical Quarterly*.

Harry Levin: from *The Overreacher: A Study of Christopher Marlowe*. Copyright 1952 by the President and Fellows of Harvard College. Reprinted by permission of Harvard University Press.

C. S. Lewis: from *Proceedings of the British Academy*, vol. XXXVIII, 1952. Copyright 1952 by the British Academy. Reprinted by permission of Oxford University Press, London, and the British Academy.

M. M. Mahood: from *Poetry and Humanism*. Copyright 1950 by M. M. Mahood. Reprinted by permission of Kennikat Press, Inc., Port Washington, N.Y.

Arthur Mizener: from *College English*, vol. V, no. 2, 1943. Copyright 1943 by the National Council of Teachers of English. Reprinted by permission of the author and the National Council of Teachers of English.

F. P. Wilson: from *Marlowe and the Early Shakespeare*. Copyright 1953 by The Clarendon Press, Oxford. Reprinted by permission of the publisher.

This anthology © 1970 by University of Miami Press
Library of Congress Catalog Card No. 69–15927
SBN 87024-121-4

CONTENTS

In the forty years that followed Marlowe's death in 1593, he was remembered quite differently by two groups of people. The poets and dramatists, some of whom had been his friends, thought of him primarily as a poet. They remembered him more for *Hero and Leander* than for his plays. Ben Jonson praised 'Marlowe's mighty line'; Michael Drayton said 'his raptures were all air and fire'; Shakespeare paid him an indirect tribute when he addressed and quoted him in *As You Like It*:

> Dead *Shepherd*, now I find thy saw of might,
> Who ever lov'd, that lov'd not at first sight?

But to those Puritan writers intent on attacking the corrupting influence of stage-plays, Marlowe's sudden and violent death seemed a clear sign that God had judged him for his atheistical views, his immoral life, and his flamboyant writing. 'He cursed and blasphemed to his last gasp'; 'he was stabbed to death by a bawdy serving man, a rival of his in his lewd love'. These were the rumours they heard and passed on, adding new details in the retelling.

After the theatres were closed in 1642 Marlowe's plays were no longer performed and by the time that Milton's nephew, Edward Phillips, was writing in 1675, Marlowe's reputation as a dramatist had come to an end and he was virtually forgotten until well on into the eighteenth century. Even at the end of the eighteenth century, Thomas Warton could be astonished that *Dr Faustus* had ever 'had possession of the public theatres of our metropolis'. This play 'now only frightens children at a puppet-show in a county-town'.

In 1744 Robert Dodsley included *Edward II* in his *Select Collection of Old Plays*. This was the first publication of any authentic work by Marlowe since the last edition of *Hero and Leander* in 1637. Dodsley went on to publish the *Jew of Malta* in 1780; C. W. Dilke published *Dr Faustus* in 1814; *Hero and Leander* was published in 1815 and *Tamburlaine* in 1818. This was the year that the actor Edmund Kean revived *The Jew of Malta*—the first performance of any of Marlowe's plays for 155 years. From this point onwards there was an increasing interest in Marlowe. Hazlitt and Broughton both made attempts to rescue him from critical neglect. Broughton questioned the accuracy of the still persistent rumours about his death. He wrote to the vicar at Deptford to find the record of Marlowe's burial and received the reply that he was 'slain by ffrancis Archer'. This was odd; Vaughan, writing in 1600, had said that the slayer's name was 'one . . . Ingram'. Nevertheless, the vicar's reading of 'Archer' became generally accepted for the next hundred years.

In Hazlitt we see the first signs of the 'romantic' view of Marlowe as the daring, imaginative and unshackled genius of the Renaissance. This romantic view became a passionate enthusiasm later in the nineteenth century with Taine, Swinburne and Havelock Ellis. 'He first, and he alone, gave wings to English poetry; he first brought into its serene and radiant atmosphere the new strange element of sublimity'; 'he is his own hero'. U. M. Ellis-Fermor, writing in 1927, represents perhaps the furthest extreme of this line of criticism: 'He strips away all that might cloud or deflect the vision and forces us to look at man face to face with God... He leads us to a realization that dazzles and stupefies by its absoluteness and its finality.' William Empson, Paul Kocher, Harry Levin and E. M. Waith are more sensitive and sophisticated critics in this same general tradition; they see Marlowe as a Renaissance hero questioning traditional morality and reaching out to new possibilities of human endeavour and experience. Levin's work, in particular, is always illuminating.

Meanwhile, in 1925, a young American scholar, J. Leslie Hotson, made a series of remarkable discoveries in London that completely changed the traditional picture of how Marlowe had met his death. Hotson had been puzzling over the name of Marlowe's killer. Was it 'ffrancis Archer' or 'Ingram'? He looked for himself at the Deptford burial record and discovered that the vicar who replied to Broughton in 1830 had misread the handwriting. The correct reading was 'slaine by ffrancis ffrezer'. Hotson concluded that 'there never was an Archer who had anything to do with Marlowe's death'. Was the slayer then 'Ingram' or 'Francis Frezer'? Hotson was looking through some Elizabethan documents in the Public Records office in Chancery Lane. 'As I turned over the leaves of the Calendar of Close Rolls, my eye fell upon the name *Ingram Frizer*. I felt at once that I had come upon the man who killed Christopher Marlowe.' He searched through the records and at last discovered that 'Ingram Frisar' was granted a pardon on June 28, 1593 for killing Marlowe in self-defence a month earlier. Finally, he found the writ and inquisition in Chancery, giving a full report of the coroner's inquest. Hotson's brilliant piece of detection established the true facts of Marlowe's death and showed conclusively that the 'lewd love', the 'low resort', and the 'bawdy serving man' were all misleading rumours.

Leslie Hotson's biographical research was supplemented by Ethel Seaton, who discussed the use Marlowe made of the books he had read, and by several other writers (Mark Eccles and William Urry for example) who over the past thirty years have filled in some of the details of Marlowe's little-known life. Besides these scholars there have been those interested in solving the textual problems presented by the plays themselves. The most important contribution here since the six volume edition under the general editorship of R. H. Case, 1930-33, is W. W. Greg's edition of the parallel texts of *Dr Faustus*, 1604-16, and his conjectural reconstruction of the play, both published in 1950.

Dr Faustus is the play that has aroused the most discussion and controversy amongst critics over the past thirty years and the student of Marlowe could well begin by thinking about the meaning of this play. James M. Smith's article of 1939 deals with the allegorical implications of *Dr Faustus*; Arthur Mizener discusses the dualistic view of the world implicit in the play; W. W. Greg and Leo Kirschbaum see it as a morality play; Nicholas Brooke regards it as an 'inverted morality'; and Jerzy Grotowski's odd but stimulating production of the play in Poland carries the 'inverted morality' interpretation about as far as it will go. Lily B. Campbell's essay of 1952 treats *Dr Faustus* as a 'case of conscience', a product more of the Reformation than of the Renaissance, with despair as Faustus's chief sin; and D. J. Palmer examines the texture of the poetry and its transforming power of illusion. Although we have the space to print only three of these eight essays in our book, we have given details of the others in the bibliography so that students who are interested can find and read them for themselves. This collection at least provides a starting point and a guide to further reading and thinking about Marlowe.

Cambridge, 1968   *Judith O'Neill*

NOTE: In the different editions of Marlowe's plays, the characters appear variously as Abigail or Abigall, Isabel or Isabella, Mephistopholis, Mephostophilis or Mephastophilis etc. In each essay printed here we have preserved the spelling of whichever edition the critic has chosen to use.

Critics on Marlowe: 1592-1930

ROBERT GREENE (1560?-92)

Wonder not ... thou famous gracer of Tragedians [i.e. Marlowe], that Greene, who hath said with thee (like the foole in his heart), There is no God, shoulde now give glorie unto his greatnesse: for penetrating is his power, his hand lyes heavie upon me, hee has spoken unto me with a voice of thunder, and I have felt he is a God that can punish enemies. Why should thy excellent wit, his gift, bee so blinded that thou shouldst give no glorie to the giver? Is it pestilent Machivilian pollicy that thou hast studied? O peevish follie. What are his rules but meere confused mockeries, able to extirpate in small time the genera-tions of mankind. ... Delight not (as I have done) in irreligious oaths. ... Despise drunkenes which wasteth the wit and maketh men all equal unto beasts. Flie lust, as the death'sman of the soule; ... Abhor those Epicures, whose loose life hath made religion lothsome to your eyes; and when they sooth you with tearms of Maistership, remember *Robert Greene*, whom they have often so flattered, perishes now for want of comfort! ... The fire of my life is now at the last snuffe. ... Trust not, then (I beseech ye) to such weake staies for they are as changeable in mind, as in many attyres.

'Desirous that you should live though himself be dying'
Robert Greene

Groatsworth of Wit bought with a Million of Repentence, 1592, The Bodley Head Quartos, ed. G. B. Harrison, London, 1923, pp. 43-4, 46-7.

RICHARD BAINES (died 1594?)

That the Indians and many Authors of Antiquitei have assuredly written of about 16 thowsande yeers agone, wher Adam is proved to have leyved within 6 thowsande yeers.

He affirmeth That Moyses was but a Juggler, and that one Heriots can do more than hee.

That Moyses made the Jewes to travell fortie yeers in the wildernes (which iorny might have ben don in lesse than one yeer) er they came to the promised lande, to the intente that those who were privei to most of his subtileteis might perish, and so an everlastinge supersticion remayne in the hartes of the people.

That the firste beginnynge of Religion was only to keep men in awe.

That it was an easye matter for Moyses, beinge brought up in all the artes of the Egiptians, to abuse the Jewes, being a rude and grosse people.

That Christ was a Bastard, and his mother dishonest.

That he was the sonne of a carpenter, and that, yf the Jewes amonge whome he was borne did crucifye him, thei best knew him and whence he came.

That Christ deserved better to dye than Barrabas, and that the Jewes made a good choyce, though Barrabas were both a theife and a murtherer.

That yf ther be any God or good Religion, then it is in the Papistes, because the service of God is performed with more ceremonyes, as elevacion of the masse, organs, singinge men, *shaven crownes,* &c. That all protestantes ar hipocriticall Asses.

That, yf he wer put to write a new religion, he wolde undertake both a more excellent and more admirable methode, and that all the new testament is filthely written.

That the Women of Samaria wer whores, and that Christ knew them dishonestlye.

That St John the Evangelist was bedfellowe to Christe, that he leaned alwayes in his bosom, that he used him as the synners of Sodome.

That all thei that love not tobacco and boyes are fooles.

That all the Appostells wer fishermen and base fellowes, neither of witt nor worth, that Pawle only had witt, that he was a timerous fellow in biddinge men to be subiect to magistrates against his conscience.

That he had as good right to coyne as the Queen of Englande, and that he was acquainted with one Poole, a prisoner in newgate, whoe hath great skill in mixture of metalls, and havinge learned such thinges of him, he ment, through help of a cunnynge stampe-maker, to coyne french crownes, pistolettes, and englishe shillinges.

That, yf Christ had instituted the Sacramentes with more cerymony-all reverence, it would have ben had in more admiracion, that it wolde have ben much better beinge administered in a Tobacco pype.

That the Angell Gabriell was Bawde to the holy Ghoste, because he brought the salutation to Marie.

That one Richard Cholmelei hath confessed that he was perswaded by Marloes reason to become an Athieste.

Theis thinges, with many other, shall by good and honest men be proved to be his opinions and common specches, and that this Marloe doth not only holde them himself, but almost in every company he commeth, perswadeth men to Athiesme willinge them not to be afrayed of bugbeares and hobgoblins and utterly scornynge both God and his ministers....

I thincke, all men in christianitei ought to endevor that the mouth of so dangerous a member may be stopped....

A Note Contayninge the Opinion of one Christofer Marlye, Concernynge his Damnable Opinions and Judgment of Relygion and Scorne of Gods Worde, 1593, MS. Harl. 6853, Fol. 320. The original title has been partly scored through with a pen and altered as follows: *A Note delivered on Whitson eve last of the most horreble blasphemes utteryd by Christofer Marly who within iii dayes after came to a soden and fearful end of his life.* This Note is reprinted in full in (among other places) Havelock Ellis's edition of Marlowe's Works in 1887, pp. 428-9. Havelock Ellis gives the author's name as 'Bame' but Baines is the more usual reading. The words printed in italics have been scored through in the MS. See Joseph Ritson, p. 15 of this present book.

GEORGE PEELE (1558?–97?)

> ...unhappy in thine end,
> Marley, the Muses' darling for thy verse,
> Fit to write passions for the souls below,
> If any wretched souls in passion speak.

The Prologue to *The Honours of the Garter*, 1593, in *The Works of George Peele*, Now first collected with some account of his writings and notes by the Rev. Alexander Dyce, London, 1828, vol. II, pp. 140–1.

THOMAS BEARD (died 1632)

Not inferior to any of the former in Atheisme and impietie, and equall to all in maner of punishment, was one of our own nation, of fresh and late memorie, called Marlin [Marlowe], by profession a scholler, brought up from his youth in the Universitie of Cambridge, but by practise a Play-maker, and a Poet of scurrilitie, who by giving too large a swinge to his owne wit, and suffering his lust to have the full reines, fell (not without just desert) to that outrage and extremitie, that he denied God and his sonne Christ, and not only in word blasphemed the Trinitie, but also (as it is credibly reported) wrote bookes against it, affirming our Savior to be but a deceiver, and Moses to be but a conjurer and seducer of the people, and the holy Bible to be but vaine and idle stories, and all religion but a device of policie. But see what a hooke the Lord put in the nostrils of this barking dogge: it so fell out, that as he purposed to stab one whom he ought a grudge unto with his dagger, the other partie perceiving, so avoided the stroke, that withall catching hold of his wrest, he stabbed his owne dagger into his owne head, in such sort, that notwithstanding all the means of surgery that could be wrought, he shortly after died thereof: the manner of his death being so terible (for he even cursed and blasphemed to his last gaspe, and together with his breath an oath flew out of his mouth) that it was not only a manifest signe of God's Judgement, but also an horrible and fearfull terror to all that beheld him.

Theatre of God's Judgments, London, 1597, chap. 23, p. 149.

FRANCIS MERES (1565–1647)

As Iodelle, a French tragicall poet beeing an Epicure, and an Atheist, made a pitifull end: so our tragicall poet *Marlow* for his Epicurisme and Atheisme had a tragicall death; you may read of this *Marlow* more at large in the *Theatre of God's Judgment*. . . . As the poet Lycophron was shot to death by a certain rival of his: so *Christopher Marlow* was stabbed to death by a bawdy serving man, a rivall of his in his lewde love.

> *Palladis Tamia, Wits Treasury, Being the Second Part of Wits Commonwealth*, London, 1598, Scholars' Facsimiles and Reprints, New York, 1938, pp. 286 verso and 287 recto.

WILLIAM VAUGHAN (1577–1641)

Not inferior to these, was one Christopher Marlow, by profession a play-maker, who, as it is reported, about 14 yeares a-goe wrote a Booke againste the Trinitie; but see the effects of God's justice; it so hapned that at Detford, a little village about three miles distant from London, as he meant to stab with his ponyard one named Ingram, that had invited him thither to a feast, and was then playing at tables, hee quickly perceiving it, so avoydede the thrust, that withall drawing out his dagger for his defence, hee stabbed this Marlowe in the eye, in such sort, that his braynes coming out at the daggers point, hee shortly after dyed. Thus did God, the true executioner of divine justice, worke the ende of impious atheists.

> *The Golden-grove, moralized in three bookes*, 1600, London, 2nd ed. 1608, chap. 3, 'Of Atheists'.

EDMUND RUDIERDE (writing in 1618)

We read of one *Marlin*, a *Cambridge* Scholler, who was a Poet, and a filthy Play-maker, this wretch accounted that meeke servant of God Moses to be but a Conjurer, and our sweete Saviour but a seducer, and a deceiver of the people. But hearken ye braine-sicke and prophane

Poets and Players, that bewitch idle eares with foolish vanities: what fell upon this prophane wretch, having a quarrell against one whom he met in a streete in London and would have stabd him: But the partie perceiving his villainy prevented him with catching his hand, and turning his owne dagger into his braines, and so blaspheming and cursing, he yeelded up his stinking breath: marke this yee Players, that live by making fooles laugh at sinne and wickednesse.

> *The Thunderbolt of God's Wrath Against Hard Hearted and Stiff Necked Sinners*, London, 1618, chap. XXII, Of Epicures and Atheists, p. 29.

MICHAEL DRAYTON (1563–1631)

> Neat *Marlowe* bathed in the Thespian springs
> Had in him those brave translunary things
> That the first Poets had, his raptures were
> All ayre and fire, which made his verses cleere,
> For that fine madness still he did retaine,
> Which rightly should possesse a Poets braine.

To Henry Reynolds, 'Of Poets and Poesie', 1627, in *Works*, ed. J. William Hebel, Oxford, 1923, vol. III, pp. 226–31.

WILLIAM PRYNNE (1600–69)

[I can tell of] the visible apparition of the Devill on the Stage at the Belsavage Play-house in Queen Elizabeth's dayes (to the great amazement both of the Actors and Spectators) whiles they were there prophanely playing the History of Faustus (the truth of which I have heard from many now alive, who well remember it) there being some distracted with that fearfull sight.

> *Histrio-Mastix, The Players Scourge, or Actors Tragedie*, London, 1633, Act 6, Scene 19, p. 556.

EDWARD PHILLIPS (1630–96)

Christopher Marlow, a kind of second Shakespeare (whose contemporary he was), not only because like him he rose from an Actor to be a maker of plays, though inferior both in Fame and Merit; but also because in his begun poem of *Hero and Leander*, he seems to have a resemblance of that clear and unsophisticated Wit, which is natural to that incomparable Poet; this Poem being left unfinished by *Marlow*, who in some riotous Fray came to an untimely and violent End. . . . Of all that he hath written for the Stage his *Dr Faustus* hath made the greatest noise with its Devils and such like Tragical sport.

> *Theatrum Poetarum*, London, 1675, Part II, 'The Modern Poets', pp. 24–5.

ANTHONY a WOOD (1632–95)

Christop. Marlo, sometimes a Student in Cambridge; afterwards, first an actor on the stage, then (as Shakespeare, whose contemporary he was) a maker of Plays, tho' inferior both in fancy and merit.... But in the end, so it was, that this *Marlo* giving too large a swing to his own wit, and suffering his lust to have the full reins, fell to that outrage and extremity, as Jodelle a French tragical Poet did, (being an Epicure and an Atheist) that he denied God and his Son Christ, and not only in word blasphemed the *Trinity,* but also ... wrote divers discourses against it, affirming our *Saviour* to be a deceiver and Moses to be a conjurer: the holy Bible also to contain only vain and idle stories, and all religion but a device of policy. But see the end of this person.... For it so fell out, that he being deeply in love with a certain Woman, had for his Rival a bawdy servingman, one rather fit to be a Pimp, than an ingenious *Amoretto* as *Marlo* conceived himself to be. Whereupon *Marlo* taking it to be an high affront, rushed in upon, to stab, him, with his dagger: But the servingman being very quick, so avoided the stroke, that with all catching hold of *Marlo's* wrist, he stab'd his own dagger into his own head, in such sort, that notwithstanding all the means of surgery that could be wrought, he shortly after died of his wound, before the year 1593.

Athenae Oxonienses, London, 1691, vol. I, col. 288–9.

THOMAS WARTON (1728–90)

His tragedies manifest traces of a just dramatic conception, but they abound with tedious and uninteresting scenes, or with such extravagancies as proceeded from a want of judgment, and those barbarous ideas of the times....

Marlowe's wit and spriteliness of conversation had often the unhappy effect of tempting him to sport with sacred subjects; more perhaps from the preposterous ambition of courting the casual applause of profligate and unprincipled companions, than from any systematic disbelief of religion. His scepticism, whatever it might be, was construed by the prejudiced and peevish puritans into absolute atheism, and they took pains to represent the unfortunate catastrophe of his untimely death, as an immediate judgment from heaven upon his execrable impiety....

One of Marlowe's tragedies is *The Tragical History of the Life and Death of Doctor John Faustus*: a proof of the credulous ignorance which still prevailed and a specimen of the subjects which then were thought not improper for tragedy. A tale which at the close of the sixteenth century had the possession of the public theatres of our metropolis, now only frightens children at a puppet-show in a county-town....

The History of English Poetry, London, 1781, vol. III, pp. 453–7.

JOSEPH RITSON (1752-1803)

A great deal has been said about Marlow, his opinions and exit, from age to age; from Beard to Warton; the oldest writers ('prejudiced and peevish puritans') directly arraigning him of atheism and blasphemy; and those of more modern times (pious and orthodox churchmen) generously labouring to rescue his character, either by boldly denying or artfully extenuating the crimes alleged against him; but not an *iota* of evidence has been produced on either side. I have a great respect for Marlow as an ingenious poet, but I have a much higher regard for truth and justice; and will therefore take the liberty to produce the strangest (if not the whole) proof that now remains of his diabolical tenets and debauched morals; and if you, Mr Warton, still choose to think him innocent of the charge, I shall be very glad to see him thoroughly whitewashed in your next edition. The paper is transcribed from an old manuscript in the Harleian library . . . and was never before printed. [The 'Baines Note' then follows. See pp. 9-11.]

> *Observations on The Three First Volumes of the History of English Poetry in a Familiar Letter to the Author*, London, 1782, p. 40.

CHARLES LAMB (1775-1834)

I had . . . difficulty . . . in culling a few sane lines from this . . . play *Tamburlaine*. The lunes of *Tamburlaine* are perfect 'midsummer madness'. Nebuchadnazar's [sic] are mere modest pretensions compared with the thundering vaunts of this Scythian Shepherd. He comes . . . drawn by conquered kings and reproaches these *pampered jades of Asia* that they can *draw but twenty miles a day*. Till I saw this passage with my own eyes, I never believed that it was anything more than a pleasant burlesque of Mine Ancients'. But I assure my readers that it is soberly set down in a play which their ancestors took to be serious. . . .

Edward II is in a very different style from 'mighty Tamburlaine'. The reluctant pangs of abdicating Royalty in Edward furnished hints which Shakespeare scarce improved on in his Richard the Second; and the death-scene of Marlowe's king moves pity and terror beyond any scene, ancient or modern with which I am acquainted. . . .

Barabas is a mere monster, brought in with a large painted nose, to please the rabble. He kills in sport, poisons whole nunneries, invents infernal machines. . . . It is curious to see a superstition wearing out. The idea of a Jew (which our pious ancestors contemplated with such horror) has nothing in it now revolting. We have tamed the claws of the beast and pared its nails. . . .

The growing horrors of Faustus are awfully marked by the hours and half hours as they expire and bring him nearer and nearer to the exactment of his dire compact. It is indeed an agony and bloody sweat. ... Marlowe is said to have been tainted with atheistical positions, to have denied God and the Trinity. To such a genius the history of Faustus must have been delectable food; to wander in fields where curiosity is forbidden to go, to approach the dark gulf near enough to look in, to be busied in speculations which are the rottenest part of the core of the fruit that fell from the tree of knowledge.

Specimens of English Dramatic Poets, London, 1808, repr. 1844, vol. I, pp. 17–18, 26, 29, 37–8.

NATHAN DRAKE (1766–1836)

Marlowe, Christopher, as an author, an object of great admiration and encomium in his own times, and of all the dramatic poets who preceded Shakespeare, certainly the one who possessed the most genius. He was egregiously misled, however, by bad models, and his want of taste has condemned him, as a writer for the stage, to an obscurity from which he is not likely to emerge.

Of *Tamburlaine* ... it is impossible to speak without a mixture of wonder and contempt; for, whilst a few passages indicate talents of no common order, the residue is a tissue of unmingled rant, absurdity, and fustian: yet strange as it may appear, the most extravagent flights of this eccentric composition were the most popular, and numerous allusions to its moon-struck reveries are to be found in the productions of its times. ...

Edward the Second is a proof, that, when Marlowe chose to drop the barbarities of his age ... he could exert an influence over the heart which has not often been excelled. There is a truth, simplicity, and moral feeling in this play which irresistibly attracts, and would fain induce us to hope, that its author could not have exhibited the impious and abandoned traits of character which have usually been attributed to him. The death-scene of Edward is a master-piece of pity and terror.

The Tragical Historie of the Life and Death of Dr Faustus ... in point of preternatural wildness, and metaphysical horror, is the *chef d'oevre* of Marlowe. It unfolds not only genius of a sublimated and exotic cast, but seems to have been the product of a mind inflamed by unhallowed curiosity, and an eager irreligious desire of invading the secrets of another world, and so far gives credence to the imputations which have stained the memory of its author; for this play breathes not a poetic preternaturalism, if we may use the expression, but looks like the creature of an atmosphere emerging from the gulph of lawless spirits, and vainly employed in pursuing the corruscations which traverse its illimitable gloom.

The catastrophe of this play makes the heart shudder, and the hair involuntarily start erect; and the agonies of Faustus on the fast approaching expiration of his compact with the Devil, are depicted with a strength truly appalling.

Yet amidst all this diabolism, there occasionally occur passages of great moral sublimity, passages on which Milton seems to have fixed his eyes.... The death of Marlowe ... was violent and premature, the melancholy termination of a life rendered still more melancholy by vice and infidelity.

Shakespeare and His Times, London, 1817, vol. II, pp. 245-9.

WILLIAM HAZLITT (1778-1830)

There is a lust of power in his writings, a hunger and thirst after unrighteousness, a glow of the imagination, unhallowed by anything but its own energies. His thoughts burn within him like a furnace with bickering flames; or throwing out black smoke and mists, that hide the dawn of genius, or like a poisonous mineral, corrode the heart. His *Life and Death of Dr Faustus,* though an imperfect and unequal performance, is his greatest work. Faustus himself is a rude sketch, but it is a gigantic one. This character may be considered as the personification of the pride of will and eagerness of curiosity, sublimed beyond the reach of fear and remorse....

I cannot find, in Marlowe's play, any proofs of the atheism or impiety attributed to him, unless the belief in witchcraft and the Devil can be regarded as such; and at the time he wrote, not to have believed in both, would have been construed into the rankest atheism and irreligion. There is a delight, as Mr Lamb says, in dallying with interdicted subjects; but that does not, by any means, imply either a practical or speculative disbelief of them....

I do not think *The Rich Jew of Malta* so characteristic a specimen of this writer's powers. It has not the same fierce glow of passion or expression. It is extreme in act, and outrageous in plot and catastrophe; but it has not the same vigorous filling up.... It is a tissue of gratuitous, unprovoked, and incredible atrocities, which are committed, one upon the back of the other, by the parties concerned, without motive, passion, or object....

Edward II is, according to the modern standard of composition, Marlowe's best play. It is written with few offences against the common rules, and in a succession of smooth and flowing lines. The poet however succeeds less in the voluptuous and effeminate descriptions which he here attempts, than in the more dreadful and violent bursts of passion.... But the death of Edward II in Marlowe's tragedy, is certainly superior to that of Shakespeare's King in *Richard II*; and in heart-breaking distress, and the sense of human weakness, claiming pity from utter helplessness and conscious misery, is not surpassed by any writer whatever.

Lectures on the Dramatic Literature of the Age of Elizabeth,

1820, in *The Collected Works of William Hazlitt*, ed. A. R. Waller, and Arnold Glover, London, 1902, vol. V, pp. 202, 207, 209, 211.

JAMES BROUGHTON (Writing 1830)

The character of Edward is admirably drawn; his infatuated attachment to his worthless minions, his imbecility, his indecision, his bursts of passion, his arrogance in prosperity and abject prostration in adversity, are severally depicted with an adherence to nature and a boldness of colouring which ... places Marlowe in the first class of dramatic writer. ...

I here take my leave of Marlowe and his productions. That my feeble arguments will suffice wholly to wipe from his memory the stigma with which for upwards of two centuries it has been branded, I cannot so far flatter myself as to suppose. Many ... will doubtless remain unconvinced; while others ... will continue to take for granted the current tale of his enormities. ... My end, however, will be accomplished, should but some few be induced to pause ere they condemn him.

Series of five articles on Marlowe's life and works in *Gentleman's Magazine,* vol. C, no. I, 1830, pp. 3ff., 121ff., 222ff., 313ff., 593ff. These extracts pp. 593–7.

HENRY HALLAM (1777–1859)

If Marlowe did not re-establish blank verse, which is difficult to prove, he gave it at least a variety of cadence, and an easy adaption of the rhythm to the sense, by which it instantly became in his hands the finest instrument that the tragic poet has ever employed for his purpose. ... No-one could think of disputing the superiority of Marlowe to all his contemporaries of this early school of English drama.

Introduction to the Literature of Europe in the Fifteenth, Sixteenth and Seventeenth Centuries, London, 1834, vol. II, p. 375.

J. H. LEIGH HUNT (1784–1859)

If ever there was a born poet, Marlowe was one. He perceived things in their spiritual as well as material relations and impressed them with a corresponding felicity. Rather, he struck them as with something sweet and glowing that rushes by; perfumes from a censer, glances of love and beauty. And he could accumulate images into as deliberate and lofty a grandeur. ...

But this happy genius appears to have had as unhappy a will, which obscured his judgment. It made him condescend to write fustian for the town, in order to rule over it; subjected him to the charge of impiety, probably for nothing but too scornfully treating irreverent notions of the Deity; and brought him, in the prime of his life, to a violent end in a tavern. His plays abound in wilful and self-worshipping speeches, and every one of them turns upon some kind of ascendency at the expense of other people. . . .

Marlowe and Spenser are the first of our poets who perceived the beauty of words . . . as a habit of the poetic mood, and as receiving and reflecting beauty through the feeling of the ideas. . . .

Marlowe, although he was scholar, cared no more for geography and consistent history than Shakespeare. He took the world as he found it at the theatre, where it was a mixture of golden age innocence, tragical enormity, and a knowledge superior to all petty and transitory facts.

Imagination and Fancy; Selections from the English Poets, London, 1844, 2nd ed. 1845, pp. 136-7, 141, 143.

ALEXANDER DYCE (1798-1869)

With very little discrimination of character, with much extravagance of incident, with no pathos where pathos was to be expected, and with a profusion of inflated language, *Tamburlaine* is nevertheless a very impressive drama, and undoubtedly superior to all the English tragedies which preceded it; superior to them in the effectiveness with which the events are brought out, in the poetic feeling which animates the whole, and in the nerve and variety of the versification. . . .

Though immeasurably superior to the dramatists of his time, he is, like them, a very unequal writer; it is in detached passages and single scenes, rather than in any of his pieces taken as a whole, that he displays the vast richness and vigour of his genius. . . . For my own part, I feel a strong persuasion, that with added years and well-directed efforts, he would have made a much nearer approach in tragedy to Shakespeare than has yet been made by any of his countrymen.

The Works of Christopher Marlowe with Notes and Some Account of His Life and Writings, London, 1850, vol. I, pp. xv, lxviii.

HIPPOLYTE TAINE (1828-93)

Celui-ci [Marlowe] était un esprit déréglé, débordé, outrageusement véhément et audacieux, mais grandiose et sombre, avec la véritable fureur poétique, païen de plus, et révolté de moeurs et de doctrines. . . . Marlowe . . . est un incrédule, nie Dieu et le Christ, blasphème la Trinité . . . et dans chaque compagnie où il va, prêche son athéisme. Voilà les colères, les témérités et les excès que la liberté de penser met dans ces esprits neufs, qui, pour la première fois après tant de siècles, osent marcher sans entraves. . . .

[On the last speech of Dr Faustus: 'Now hast thou but one fair hour to live!] Voilà l'homme vivant, agissant, naturel, personnel, non pas le symbole philosophique qu'a fait Goethe, mais l'homme primitif et vrai, l'homme emporté, enflammé, esclave de sa fougue et jouet de ses rêves, tout entier à l'instant présent, pétri de convoitises, de contradictions et de folies, qui, avec des éclats et des tressaillements, avec des cris de volupté et d'angoisse, roule, le sachant, le voulant, sur la pente et les pointes de son precipice. Tout le théâtre anglais est là, ainsi qu'une plante dans son germe, et Marlowe est à Shak[e]speare ce que Pérugin est à Raphael.

Histoire de la Littérature Anglaise, Paris, 1864, 4 vols., 2nd ed. 1866, vol. II, pp. 33–4, 48.

ALGERNON CHARLES SWINBURNE (1837–1909)

My dear Sir,

Many thanks for the very welcome gift of your beautiful and valuable edition of Marlowe. I have placed it on my shelves side by side with the three volumes of Dyce's edition which I had in my bookcase at Eton thirty years ago and more.

It has given me great interest and satisfaction to examine the way in which you have discharged your glorious task of service to so glorious a memory. . . .

Yours very faithfully,

A. C. Swinburne.

Letter to A. H. Bullen, 1885, in *Letters on the English Dramatists*, London, 1910, (20 copies only, printed for private circulation by Thomas J. Wise), p. 29.

The father of English tragedy [Marlowe] and the creator of English blank verse was . . . also the teacher and the guide of Shakespeare. . . .

Marlowe differs from such little people [Greene and Peele] not in degree, but in kind; not as an eagle differs from wrens or titmice, but as an eagle differs from frogs or tadpoles. He first, and he alone, gave wings to English poetry; he first brought into its serene and radiant atmosphere the new strange element of sublimity.

Written 1909(?), *Christopher Marlowe in Relation to Greene, Peele and Lodge*, London, 1914, (20 copies only, printed for private circulation by Thomas J. Wise), pp. 5, 16. This essay was later published in the *Fortnightly Review*, vol. 105 (O.S.) 99 (N.S.), 1916, pp. 764–9.

H. HAVELOCK ELLIS (1859-1939)

... In its later more developed form Marlowe's 'mighty line' is the chief creation of English literary art; Shakespeare absorbed it, and gave it out again with its familiar cadences in *Romeo and Juliet*, and later with many broad and lovely modifications. It has become the life-blood of our literature; Marlowe's place is at the heart of English poetry, and his pulses still thrill in our verse. . . .

With the exception of *Edward II*, which stands alone, Marlowe's dramas are mostly series of scenes held together by the poetic energy of his own dominating personality. He is his own hero, and the sanguinary Scythian utters the deepest secrets of the artist's heart. . . .

Faust is no longer [as in the Faust legend] an unintelligible magician looked at from the outside, but a living man thirsting for the infinite; the sinner becomes a hero, a Tamburlaine, no longer eager to 'ride in triumph through Persepolis', who at the thought of vaster delights has ceased to care for the finite splendours of an earthly crown. . . . Marlowe's Faustus is not impelled like the Faustus of the legend by the desire of 'worldly pleasure', nor, like Goethe's, by the vanity of knowledge; it is power, power without bound, that he desires, all that is in the world, the lust of the flesh and the lust of the eyes and the pride of life, 'a world of profit and delight, Of power, of honour, and omnipotence.' This gives him a passionate energy, an emotional sensibility which Goethe's more shifting, sceptical and complex Faust lacks. . . .

> Introduction to *The Plays of Christopher Marlowe*, ed. H. Havelock Ellis for the Mermaid Series, London, 1887, pp. xxxiii, xxxiv, xxxviii.

T. S. ELIOT (1888-1965)

... The verse accomplishments of *Tamburlaine* are notably two: Marlowe gets into blank verse the melody of Spenser, and he gets a new driving power by reinforcing the sentence period against the line period. The rapid long sentence, running line into line, in the famous soliloquies 'Nature compounded of four elements' and 'What is beauty, saith my sufferings, then?' marks the certain escape of blank verse from the rhymed couplet, and from the elegiac or rather pastoral note of Surrey, to which Tennyson returned. If you contrast these two soliloquies with the verse of Marlowe's greatest contemporary, Kyd— by no means a despicable versifier—you see the importance of the innovation :

> The one took sanctuary, and, being sent for out,
> Was murdered in Southwark as he passed
> To Greenwich, where the Lord Protector lay.

Black Will was burned in Flushing on a stage;
Green was hanged at Osbridge in Kent...

which is not really inferior to:

So these four abode
Within one house together; and as years
Went forward, Mary took another mate;
But Dora lived unmarried till her death.

TENNYSON, *Dora*

In *Faustus* Marlowe went further: he broke up the line, to a gain in intensity, in the last soliloquy; and he developed a new and important conversational tone in the dialogues of *Faustus* with the devil. *Edward II* has never lacked consideration: it is more desirable, in brief space to remark upon two plays, one of which has been misunderstood and the other underrated. These are the *Jew of Malta* and *Dido Queen of Carthage*. Of the first of these, it has always been said that the end, even the last two acts, are unworthy of the first three. If one takes the *Jew of Malta* not as a tragedy, or as a 'tragedy of blood', but as a farce, the concluding act becomes intelligible; and if we attend with a careful ear to the versification, we find that Marlowe develops a tone to suit this farce, and even perhaps that this tone is his most powerful and mature tone. I say farce, but with the enfeebled humour of our times the word is a misnomer; it is the farce of the old English humour, the terribly serious, even savage comic humour, the humour which spent its last breath in the decadent genius of Dickens....

Dido appears to be a hurried play, perhaps done to order with the *Æneid* in front of him. But even here there is progress. The account of the sack of Troy is in this newer style of Marlowe's, this style which secures its emphasis by always hesitating on the edge of caricature at the right moment:

The Grecian soldiers, tir'd with ten years war,
Began to cry, 'Let us unto our ships,
Troy is invincible, why stay we here?'...

By this, the camp was come unto the walls,
And through the breach did march into the streets,
Where, meeting with the rest, 'Kill, kill!' they cried....

And after him, his band of Myrmidons,
With balls of wild-fire in their murdering paws...

At last, the soldiers pull'd her by the heels,
And swung her howling in the empty air....

We saw Cassandra sprawling in the streets...

This is not Virgil, or Shakespeare; it is pure Marlowe. By comparing the whole speech with Clarence's dream, in *Richard III*, one acquires a little insight into the difference between Marlowe and Shakespeare:

> What scourge for perjury
> Can this dark monarchy afford false Clarence?

There, on the other hand, is what Marlowe's style could not do; the phrase has a concision which is almost classical, certainly Dantesque. Again, as often with the Elizabethan dramatists, there are lines in Marlowe, besides the many lines that Shakespeare adapted, that might have been written by either:

> If thou wilt stay,
> Leap in mine arms; mine arms are open wide;
> If not, turn from me, and I'll turn from thee;
> For though thou hast the heart to say farewell,
> I have not power to stay thee.

But the direction in which Marlowe's verse might have moved, had he not 'dyed swearing', is quite un-Shakespearian, is toward this intense and serious and indubitably great poetry which, like some great painting and sculpture attains its effects by something not unlike caricature.

'Christopher Marlowe' (1919), in *Selected Essays, New Edition*, Harcourt, Brace & World, Inc., New York, 1950, pp. 104–6.

J. LESLIE HOTSON (1897–   )

... As its chief contribution, this paper provides the authoritative answer to the riddle of Marlowe's death. We know now that he was killed by a companion of his, one Ingram Frizer, gentleman, servant to Mr. Thomas Walsingham, in the presence of two witnesses, Robert Poley and Nicholas Skeres. The testimony of these men before the Coroner's jury was that Marlowe attacked Frizer from behind, and this account was borne out to the satisfaction of the jury by the evidence of two wounds on Frizer's head. Frizer was pardoned, as having killed Marlowe in self-defence. It is important to remark that he did not forfeit the good graces of his employers, the Walsinghams, who were friends of the man whom he slew.

Marlowe died instantly. This fact destroys most of the interest in Beard's account, which builds on the assumption that the poet died a more or less lingering death, in the course of which he 'cursed and blasphemed to his last gaspe, and togither with his breath an oth flew out of his mouth. . . .'

In the light of all we have learned of Ingram Frizer, his position with the Walsinghams, his property, and his associates, it is curious to read again the passage in Francis Meres's *Palladis Tamia* which runs, 'Christopher Marlow was stabd to death by a bawdy serving man, a rivall of his in his lewde love.' Frizer was occupied with a suit in Chancery when Meres published this libel, or he might have made trouble for the ill-informed and imaginative author.

The second part of the paper makes an important addition to our knowledge of Marlowe's university career, and to our ideas of how he was occupied just before entering upon his life in London. We can now picture Shakespeare's great predecessor, supported by his former employers, the Privy Council, wresting his master's degree from the cold and hostile Cambridge authorities. Most interesting are the terms of praise which, by his services, the poet earned from Archbishop Whitgift, Lord Burghley, Lord Hunsdon, and the other great officers of England. These men knew him as discreet and useful for the secret purpose of Elizabethan government. For us, such a reputation is hardly more to his credit than the accusation of 'blasphemy' is to his discredit. To praise a man as a faithful and effective secret agent is to throw little more light on his moral nature than to damn him for a freethinker.

> *The Death of Christopher Marlowe*, The Nonesuch Press, London; Harvard University Press, Cambridge, Mass. 1925, pp. 65–7.

U. M. ELLIS-FERMOR (1894–1958)

... What was the natural bent of Marlowe's mind in his early years we may see in the rhapsodic, lyrical passages of his first play; of the perversion of that mind under the influence of contemporary scholarism and theological dogma we have no record beyond the bitter attacks on Christians in *Tamburlaine*, until we come to the picture of catastrophe and confusion in *Faustus*. *Faustus* remains, then, an almost unmatched record of spiritual tragedy in a medium capable of isolating the spiritual elements and preserving them unmixed with any of the other elements of life....

Tamburlaine was a young man's vision: 'We may become immortal like the gods'; *Faustus* is an intense and passionate expression of the despair that follows upon the clouding-over of the vision of 'the face of God,' whose loss made all places hell. And so perhaps our second impression of *Faustus*, after that of the clear, uncomplicated passion of loss, is of a purely negative play, which is often only a denial or condemnation of the aspirations of *Tamburlaine*....

The character of Faustus, it cannot be too often repeated, is not that of one man, but of man himself, of Everyman. There are no details, no personal traits, no eccentricities or habits, nothing that is intimate or individual. Marlowe could not have told us where, or in what way, Faustus differed from any other man. He was concerned only with that part of him which was common to all men, yet in virtue of which he exceeded all men, his mind. And that mind—we have met it already in an earlier play—is Marlowe's. The limitless desire, the unbridled passion for the infinite, a certain reckless, high confidence in the will and spirit of man are all there as before. Throughout the earlier scenes the mind of Faustus is still 'lift upward and divine,' still 'climbing after knowledge infinite.' There are in Faustus dignity, patience, tenacity and a certain profundity of thought that are not to be found in Tamburlaine. . . . But these are only attributes of Marlowe grown older. This rare power of abstracting the nature of man, of revealing only the universal and the general, yet so revealing it that it comes home to the heart of every individual man, reaches its height at the end of the play. . . .

From the plays of Shakespeare alone we could reconstruct with comparative vividness the life of the age in which he lived. . . . But, leaving aside the question of the smaller quantity of Marlowe's work, it would go ill with the man who tried to compile from the nine extant plays a picture of 'Marlowe's England'. He is native rather to a country in which the voyages of Marco Polo, the conquests of the Great Cham, the wrestling of the souls of men with devils, are everyday events. His mind is withdrawn and travels upon a way of its own. Almost we may say of it that this way is 'hidden with God'.

But if we are content instead to follow Marlowe's mind upon its own course of thought we are amazed, not at the impressions and experiences that left no mark upon him, but at the depth of his understanding of certain issues that touch man's life nearer the root than do the material interests of the everyday world. It is true that, for many years, Marlowe is unable to analyse or re-create the character of an individual man, or to tell us anything of the complexity of his relations with other men. But in that deeper, inner world where not men's differences but their common and essential likeness is in question, he moves as a master. He considers in man not the subtle distinctions and varying relationships that mark him off from other men or bind him to them, but the immutable element in man, the spirit of man which can be matched against the universe; and here his voice has authority. He strips away all that might cloud or deflect the vision and forces us to look at man face to face with God, where no other man can stand beside him. So almost impossible a task is this that the mind falters before it. He leads us to a realization that dazzles and stupefies by its absoluteness and its finality. He forces upon the consciousness of his readers, by an intensity which there is no gainsaying, naked truth, which is yet too simple to be apprehended. . . .

Christopher Marlowe, Methuen, London, 1927. Reprinted by Archon Books, Hamden, Conn., 1967, pp. 66, 84–5, 134–5.

C. F. TUCKER BROOKE (1883–1946)

... Few poets certainly have paralleled the ability which Marlowe shows in his early plays of condensing an entire lyric into a single glorious verse. In *Tamburlaine* and *Faustus* particularly, the splendid scenes as they unroll display mighty lines which glitter and writhe like burnished living serpents. Sometimes the reader is shaken into breathlessness by ten syllables that reveal the wild strange beauty of a yearning soul:

> 'Was this the face that launched a thousand ships?'
> 'Tis magic, magic, that has ravished me.'
> 'And ride in triumph through Persepolis.'
> 'The sweet fruition of an earthly crown.'
> 'Still climbing after knowledge infinite.'
> 'Infinite riches in a little room.'

Sometimes we are startled by the naked revelation of a mind laid bare in the moment of ultimate decision:

> 'A God is not so glorious as a king.'
> 'I'd give them all for Mephistophilis.'
> 'And all is dross that is not Helena.'

Sometimes the line becomes a paean of exulting arrogance:

> 'There is no music to a Christian's knell!'
> 'Holla ye pampered jades of Asia!'
> 'Have I not made blind Homer sing to me?'
> 'I hold the fates bound fast in iron chains.'
> 'O girl! O gold! O beauty! O my bliss!'

Again it sums up with a divine finality one of the colossal truths of human experience:

> 'For Tamburlaine, the scourge of God, must die.'
> 'Cut is the branch that might have grown full straight.'
> 'And where hell is, there must we ever be.'

And sometimes the single terrible line illumines as with white flame the soul's last effort against the inevitable:

> 'Break heart, drop blood, and mingle it with tears.'
> 'But stay awhile, let me be king till night.'
> 'I'll burn my books! Ah Mephistophilis!' ...

'Marlowe' (about 1922) in *Essays on Shakespeare and Other Elizabethans*, Yale U.P. New Haven, 1948, pp. 181–3.

... *Dido* is the only play in which Marlowe has made sexual love the real centre of the action, and it contains (at least among his plays) his most elaborate portraits of women—portraits which, despite occasional youthful blurrings of the outline, lack neither subtlety nor delicacy of feeling. It is, indeed, a spirited and moving tragedy, deserving the approval it has usually been accorded by dramatic historians; but for the student of Marlowe its value as a work of art is surpassed by its value as an index of the young poet's relation to the classics and to his profession of poetry. The most useful aesthetic criticism is therefore not that which concerns the total effect conveyed by this work of borrowed plot and rather composite style, but that which deals with the many illuminating individual passages where we see the impact of Virgil's splendid gravity upon the most exuberantly romantic of the Elizabethan dramatists, or mark the blend of ardent impulse with austere intellectual insight that best defines Marlowe's view of life. . . .

The Life of Marlowe and The Tragedy of Dido, Queen of Carthage, ed. C. F. Tucker Brooke, in R. H. Case's edition of Marlowe's *Works*, Methuen, London, 1930. Reprinted 1966 by Gordian Press, New York, p. 123.

Modern Critics on Marlowe

M. C. BRADBROOK

A Discussion of *Tamburlaine*

THE attempt to define the conventions of a particular dramatist is more difficult than to define those of a period. They will depend on the limitations of his interests and sensibility, which are disputable qualities: they will also involve a modification of the more general conventions.... The degree in which the greater writers relied upon general conventions naturally increases with the development of the drama. Marlowe had the least to rely upon: he found dramatic forms, like dramatic blank verse, stiff and inflexible; the history of his development is one of growing plasticity. He was affected by his age chiefly in matters of presentation.

The two parts of *Tamburlaine*, his earliest surviving work, illustrate a temporary equilibrium of personal and general conventions and its breakdown through Marlowe's own development. It is generally conceded that *Tamburlaine*, Part 1, has a unity of the parts with the whole which *Tamburlaine*, Part 2, does not possess, and that Marlowe attempted to do twice what could only be done once.

The unity of Part 1 is supplied by Tamburlaine himself. He is hardly thought of as a man, though it is not in Part 1 that he is most frequently equated with a god or a devil. He is a dramatic figure symbolizing certain qualities, and he defines himself in the famous 'Nature that framed us of four elements'. [All quotations are from U. M. Ellis-Fermor's edition of *Tamburlaine*, 1930] The most direct statement of his nature is, however, given by Meander.

> Some powers divine or else infernal mixed
> Their angry seeds at his conception:
> For he was never sprung of human race,
> Since with the spirit of his fearful pride
> He dares so doubtlessly resolve of rule
> And by profession be ambitious.   2. 6. 9 ff.

Tamburlaine's ambition has no definite object; it exists in and for itself. His aspiring mind is drawn upward as naturally as gravitation draws a stone downward. Herein Marlowe encounters a difficulty, for Tamburlaine's immediate aims can never be the objective correlative of this divine striving. The extraordinary drop at the end of 'Nature that framed us of four elements' to

> That perfect bliss and sole felicity
> The sweet fruition of an earthly crown   2. 7. 28 ff.

has been often observed. It is in vain that Marlowe insists that Tamburlaine despises wealth and only desires rule: earthly rule is in itself no fit equivalent for his feelings (as language has no fit expression for the divine beauty of Zenocrate). Tamburlaine is god-like ('a god is not so glorious as a king') but his accomplishments are limited to human possibilities. Marlowe escaped from the difficulty by making Tamburlaine's objects as generalized as possible, and his conquests effortless; also by formalizing the action which showed his mundane success and insisting on his contest with 'Jove' and the fates.

To generalize Tamburlaine's aims, Marlowe uses riches in their most beautiful forms, though the 'milk white harts' and 'ivory sled' of Zenocrate, the 'sun-bright armour', 'silk and cloth of gold', are in any case only symbols of the pomp of rule, of 'riding in triumph through Persepolis'. Marlowe's sensuousness has the maximum of concreteness and the minimum of particularity. The dazzling pictures of gold and jewels and the use of bright, clear colours make the impression of Tamburlaine's wealth solid enough, but it is not particularized; there are few cases where shape or outline is given to the visual image. The sonorous place-names too suggest somewhere precise; yet since they are devoid of associations for the most part, they have, as it were, a catalytic value only.

This unfocussed impressionism is helped by the firm uncolloquial movement of the 'mighty line' and by Marlowe's lack of sentence structure (e.g. in 2. 1. 7–30, 3. 2. 70–80, 5. 2. 72–128).

Tamburlaine's conquests are always quite effortless. There is no doubt in his mind, and no check in his success. He 'holds the Fates bound fast in iron chains'. The series of opponents are only a row of ninepins to be toppled over: there is no interest attached to them, except as necessary material upon which Tamburlaine can demonstrate his power. Hence the deaths of the virgins of Damascus or of Bajazet are not meant to excite sympathy or convey a feeling of physical suffering at all. (The natural callousness of the Elizabethans would make this perfectly possible.) They are not considered for themselves, but only as a means of displaying certain qualities of Tamburlaine, his absolute power and his superhuman inflexibility (for the fact that he can be indifferent to them, and even subdue his own relenting at Zenocrate's distress is a proof that he is superior to the gods. 5.2. 120 ff).

There is no hint in the verse of the physical sufferings of the virgins;

they are a set of innocent white dummies, without sticky blood like Duncan's. Their death is not shocking because it is not dramatically realized. They speak in the voices of public messengers, not of terrified women:

> Pity our plights. O pity poor Damascus!
> Pity old age. . . .
> Pity the marriage bed. . . .
>
> O then for these and such as we ourselves
> Pity, O pity, sacred Emperor.   5. 2. 17 ff.

Their acting was probably as formal as their speech.

Similarly, Bajazet's sufferings are never seen from Bajazet's point of view. His rage is a necessary proof of Tamburlaine's power, as the sufferings of the damned were popularly supposed to contribute to the glory of God: without him Tamburlaine's glory could not be demonstrated:

> Such are objects fit for Tamburlaine
> Wherein as in a mirror may be seen
> His honour, that consists in shedding blood.   5. 2. 413 ff.

Even in his love for Zenocrate Tamburlaine scarcely descends to the human level. The one episode where he shows any feeling is in dumb show (3. 2. 65). Zenocrate is much more human, and herein contrasted with him; but she thinks of Tamburlaine as half-divine. For instance, when Agydas is persuading her not to love him, the arguments are quite shrewd and incontrovertible at a naturalist level:

> How can you fancy one that looks so fierce
> Only disposed to martial stratagems?
> Who, when he shall embrace you in his arms
> Will tell how many thousand men he slew
> And when you look for amorous discourse
> Will rattle forth his facts of war and blood. . . .   3. 2. 40 ff.

It is reminiscent of Falstaff upon Hotspur. But Zenocrate does not attempt to meet Agydas at the same level of discourse. She soars over his argument and confutes him by a quite irrelevant reply.

> As looks the sun through Nilus' flowing stream
> Or when the morning holds him in her arms
> So looks my lordly love, fair Tamburlaine. . . .   3. 2. 47 ff.

This is quite a different person from Agydas's Tamburlaine: Zenocrate has dehumanized him.

Of course Tamburlaine has a human level. His irony is a personal trait. Such things as the 'pretty jest' of attacking Cosroe, the jeering repetition of Bajazet's phrase: 'Where are your *stout contributory kings*?' (3. 3. 214; cf. 3. 3. 93); and his remark to the caged Turk before he goes to fight the Soldan: 'Pray for us, Bajazet: we are going', are not very noticeable at first reading, but they became characteristic of the Marlovian villain hero, such as Aaron and Richard III.

The same kind of mordant satire can be felt in the comic episodes. Mycetes's buffoonery criticizes even the heroics of Tamburlaine himself, as later, the cynicism of Calyphas does.

> Brother Cosroe, I find myself aggrieved,
> Yet insufficient to express the same,
> For it requires a great and thundering speech.   I. I. I

This is, in its minor way, a corrective to the high-astounding terms. The peevish tone of Mycetes is sustained in a kind of nagging self-importance, sometimes emphasized by a rhymed couplet:

> O where is duty and allegiance now?
> Fled to the Caspian or the Ocean main?
> What shall I call thee: brother? no, a foe,
> Monster of nature, shame unto thy stock
> That durst presume thy sovereign for to mock!
> Meander, come: I am abused, Meander.   I. I. 101 ff.

The whining vowels of the last line make the purpose of the passage quite unmistakable. It is the same ironic spirit as Tamburlaine's 'horseplay' or Calyphas's refusal to fight.

> Go, go, tall stripling, fight you for us both:
> And take my other toward brother there....
> Take you the honour, I will take my ease.
> My wisdom shall excuse my cowardice.   Part 2, 4. I. 33 ff.

Again one is reminded of Falstaff at Shrewsbury. Of course, Tamburlaine's ideal is not seriously attacked, but these minor contrasts throw it into relief, like small touches of a contrasting colour in a painting.

The other minor characters act as foils to Tamburlaine; for example, the three followers are set against him in 2. 5. Zenocrate, though she defends the superhuman Tamburlaine, often evokes personal feelings, and those connected with human frailty.

> Ah, Tamburlaine, my love, sweet Tamburlaine
> That fightest for sceptres and for slippery crowns....
> Behold the Turk and his great emperess.   5. 2. 293–5

The dying words of Arabia are the most poignant in the play and suggest the temper of Zenocrate's own death scene in Part 2:

> Since death denies me further cause of joy
> Deprived of care, my heart with comfort dies
> Since thy desired hand shall close mine eyes.   5. 2. 367–70

The narrative is built upon a cumulative plan: Tamburlaine's enemies appear as in a Mummer's play, one down, t'other come on.

Marlowe, however, shows a growing skill in interweaving the episodes; the Soldan begins to move before Bajazet is quite finished with, so that there is not a gap between the two campaigns. Also the enemies become progressively nobler: Mycetes is a fool and Tamburlaine attacks him merely for wealth: Cosroe and Bajazet are soldiers and it is a great triumph to overcome them; the Soldan and Arabia are fighting for the person of Zenocrate.

But the actual battles are not of any great importance in Part 1; the stage directions are comparatively short, and speech is much more stressed than action, which is mostly violent and symbolic. (It should not be forgotten that the plays are styled 'The two tragicall *discourses* of Tamburlaine the Great'.)

Action is formalized for the same reason that Tamburlaine's objects are left undefined; because it is an inadequate correlative to the feeling. It tends to be on another level of interest altogether. For example, the use of the crown, and the different pieces of action concerned with it have been considered horseplay or even interpolations. But as the symbol of power and rule, the crown was often used on the Elizabethan stage in purely conventional action, which on the modern stage would appear ludicrous. In the deposition scene of *Edward II* the King removes his crown saying:

> Here, take my crown: the life of Edward, too.

But he cannot bring himself to resign it, and retracts, feeling that while he wears the crown he has power as a king.

> See, monsters, see, I'll wear my crown again.
> What, fear you not the fury of your king?

And after there is the stage direction: 'The king rageth'. He has another lengthy speech, full of hesitations.

>   Here, receive my crown,
> Receive it? no, these innocent hands of mine
> Shall not be guilty of so foul a crime:
> Take it. . . .
>   Yet stay, for rather than I'll look on them
> Here, here!   [*Gives the crown.*]

In the deposition scene of *Richard II* there is similar action; and the division of the coronet in the opening scene of *King Lear* is also relevant. If the sacred power of the crown is remembered, the struggle of Mycetes and Tamburlaine (2. 4), the similar tussle of Zabina and Zenocrate, and the final crowning of Zenocrate may be seen in a new light.

When Tamburlaine supports Cosroe, he offers him the crown which he had taken from Mycetes (at the beginning of 2. 5). Cosroe told him to keep his crown, for he had already been crowned (at 1. 1. 160) by his own followers.

Then when Tamburlaine attacks Cosroe in turn, his triumph is assured by the stage direction: 'Tamburlaine takes the crown and puts it on' (2. 7. 52).

When Tamburlaine goes to fight Bajazet he gives his crown to Zenocrate to wear while he is fighting. Bajazet gives his to Zabina and the two queens have a wordy battle while the alarums are sounded within. When the fighting is over, Tamburlaine resumes his own crown, but his followers also wrench Bajazet's from Zabina and crown him with that as well.

In 3. 3 the followers enter with the crowns of Bajazet's followers, saying:

> We have their crowns: their bodies strew the field.

These crowns they deliver up to Tamburlaine. (Compare the scene in Part 2 where they deliver their crowns to Tamburlaine in token of fealty and receive them again.)

In 4. 4 there is a 'course of crowns' brought into the banquet. (These were presumably sweetmeats shaped like crowns.) Tamburlaine says to his followers:

> Here are the cates you desire to finger, are they not?

But they refuse, saying that only kings should feed on them.

Zenocrate's coronation is reserved until Tamburlaine has greater honours to give her; it closes the play and marks his final triumph.

It is very striking that 'crown' is often used as a synonym for 'power' or 'kingdom'. The 'golden round' must have served as definite a part in the stage action as storming the tiring house, or the descent of the throne. These various incidents would obviously hang together in any stage performance and acquire a general significance.

Something similar is effected in 1. 2, where Tamburlaine first appears in 'shepherds' weeds'. Zenocrate treats him as an inferior; someone at all events who can be argued with. But Tamburlaine throws off his shepherd's clothes and puts on full armour, taking a curtle axe. The difference in appearance, when Alleyn played Tamburlaine, must have made the action easily seem symbolic. Techelles comments on it:

> As princely lions when they rouse themselves
> Stretching their paws, and threatening herds of beasts,
> So in his armour, looketh Tamburlaine.
> Methinks I see kings kneeling at his feet,
> And he with frowning brows and fiery looks
> Spurning their *crowns* from off their captive heads.   1. 2. 52 ff.

From this point Tamburlaine's accent grows even more assured than before. There is, as Miss Ellis-Fermor has noted, a development in his attitude towards himself. At first Jove is his protector; later he is a rival, even a worsted rival. The constant imagery of battle against the gods, and the relative unimportance of Tamburlaine's actual battles, keep this before the mind and prevent his desires 'lift upward and divine' from seeming to be fixed on 'the sweet fruition of an earthly *crown*'. Consider such passages as

> Our quivering lances shaking in the air
> And bullets like Jove's dreadful thunderbolts
> Enrolled in flames and fiery smouldering mists
> Shall threat the gods more than Cyclopian wars.   2. 3. 18 ff.

The play is full of such speeches wherein the actual enemy is quite lost to sight. Tamburlaine's battles are fought much more in his defiant speeches than in the 'alarums and excursions' which occasionally reproduce them at the level of the action. Hence his command to Zenocrate to 'manage words' with Zabina while he fights Bajazet seems to make her really included in the contest (besides, she is wearing his crown, as has been said, and therefore has some delegated authority). So that the issue of the flyting match is a matter for serious concern. Tamburlaine's own defiance of Bajazet and of his other enemies is similar in effect.

Tamburlaine is in fact more like a pageant than the modern idea of a play. Its central theme (Tamburlaine's 'thirst of reign') is highly generalized, its speech is uncolloquial, its feeling dehumanized and its action conventional. But this does not prevent its being a good play in the Elizabethan manner. Regarded simply as an artistic success, *Tamburlaine*, Part 1, is the most satisfactory thing Marlowe ever did, except *Hero and Leander*. But it could not be repeated. The sensuous intensity and emotional tenuity were only possible to an immature mind. Marlowe could not help developing, and so becoming more aware of personal feeling and of a wider range of sensuous impressions; he could not help his blank verse reflecting the increased development and becoming more varied and flexible too. So that in *Tamburlaine*, Part 2, he could not revive the conqueror of Part 1. The cumulative narrative could not be stretched any further, and the story of Part 2 is either a variation of Part 1 (the four kings being substituted for Bajazet) or a series of irrelevant incidents, such as those connected with Olympia. Marlowe's flagging interest is betrayed by the incorporation of passages from his current reading, in an undigested form (especially the speeches on military strategy, 3. 2). The characterization is also less consistent. Marlowe is in parts capable of a new tenderness to humanity, which does not fit in with the old figures. At the death of Zenocrate, when Tamburlaine says:

> For she is dead! thy words do pierce my soul;
> Ah, sweet Theridamus, say so no more:

> Though she be dead, yet let me think she lives,
> And feed my mind that dies for want of her—   2. 4. 125 ff.

there is, as Miss Ellis-Fermor notes, a development beyond the earlier play. Even the decision to burn the town where she died is made the occasion for a conceit which would have been out of place before, because based on a natural human grief.

> The houses, burnt, will look as if they mourned.   2. 4. 139 ff.

On the other hand the Tamburlaine of Part 2 falls below the earlier figure in some respects. His ends are more definite and less exalted. He even says:

> Cooks shall have pensions to provide us cates:
> And glut us with the dainties of the world.   1. 6. 92–3

The coarsely sensuous 'glut' indicates the new kind of feeling which has crept in. Marlowe cannot keep Tamburlaine's magnificence generalized any longer, nor can he keep the slaughter unreal and unmoving. There is a great deal of red, sticky blood in Part 2; it flows in the scene where Tamburlaine cuts his arm (3. 2. 115) and it is given through the verse. Battlefields are 'covered with a liquid purple veil' and 'sprinkled with the brains of slaughtered men' (1. 4. 80–1).

The finest passages of verse are those which point forward to *Faustus* and the later plays, or which depend on other writers—

> Helen, whose beauty summoned Greece to arms
> And drew a thousand ships to Tenedos—   2. 4. 87–8

or the reminiscence of Spenser (4. 3. 119–24). Marlowe is clearly uncertain of himself, and his verse reflects the transition. It is noticeable that he sometimes tries to pull it together by a use of strophic repetition, as in the famous 'To entertain divine Zenocrate' or the chronic lament of the three followers (5. 3) for the death of Tamburlaine. This scene opens with an echo of the earlier play.

> Now clear the triple region of the air....
> Smile, stars that reigned at my nativity
> And dim the brightness of their neighbour lamps....
>   Part 1, 4. 2. 30 ff.

reappears as

> Weep, heavens and vanish into liquid tears!
> Fall, stars that govern his nativity
> And summon all the shining lamps of heaven
> To cast their bootless fires to the earth....

Each of the three kings speaks in turn, and each speech ends with a rhymed couplet. The same kind of pattern appears at the level of action in the scenes where the three kings deliver their crowns up to Tamburlaine (1. 4, 5): it is very like the entries of the lords in 3 *Henry VI*, 5.1.

There is on the whole little symbolic action in Part 2, the particular equipoise which made it possible in Part 1 having been destroyed. In his next play, Marlowe took a different type of narrative, and constructed his play in quite another fashion. . . .

From Chapter VI of *Themes and Conventions of Elizabethan Tragedy*, C.U.P., Cambridge, 1935, pp. 137–48.

HELEN GARDNER

The Second Part of
Tamburlaine the Great

Criticism has been harsh to the second of Marlowe's plays on the career of Tamburlaine. It is usually regarded as an inferior sequel to the first part, repeating its theme with a different ending. Some critics have seen in it a study of degeneration, a picture of the great adventurer of the first part growing more bloodthirsty, cruel and boastful, until, at the height of his triumphs, he is cut off. Miss Ellis-Fermor, in her edition of both parts, feels that the second is very different from the first and ascribes this difference to a change in Marlowe's feeling towards his hero; but she feels that the result of this change is boredom with his theme and imaginative poverty in handling it. 'Of the events and episodes available to Marlowe when he wrote the first part of *Tamburlaine*,' she writes, 'very few had been omitted. There was, consequently, little left of the original legend when a second part was to be written. He had, beyond doubt, a clear conception of the development the chief character should suffer, and this differed so far from the conception of the first part as to endanger the effectiveness of a play written on similar lines. . . . In this situation, then, with his sources for the life already drained and his sympathies no longer strongly enough engaged to stimulate his imagination to constructive plotting, he seems to have been driven to eke out his material by introducing irrelevant episodes, some of which he weaves in skilfully, others of which are, and look like, padding. . . . The first part alone reveals Marlowe's mind at work on a characteristic structure; much of the second, though flashes of power and passages of thought as clear as anything in the earlier part occur at intervals throughout, is, by comparison, journeyman work. The form of the whole is no longer an inevitable expression of an underlying idea.'[1]

It is the argument of this article that the second part of *Tamburlaine* has been misjudged and that while it is true that Marlowe's sympathies have changed since he wrote the first part, it is not true that this makes his play ineffective, since the change of sympathies has meant a change of theme, and the change of theme has, in turn, necessitated a change of structure. The second part of *Tamburlaine* is not a mere

---

[1] *Tamburlaine the Great*, edited by U. M. Ellis-Fermor, London, 1930, pp. 41 and 46. All quotations from *Tamburlaine* are taken from this edition.

continuation of the first; it is different in intention and plan. The sub-sidiary episodes, which seem irrelevant padding if we regard the play as a rewriting of the first part with a different ending, are relevant when we recognize the theme and the play's structure. It cannot be claimed that the second part of *Tamburlaine* is a great play, but it can be claimed that it is better than it is commonly supposed to be, and that it shows in some degree the Shakespearian method of plotting, in which episodes and sub-plots are linked to the main plot by idea, rather than the primitive structure of *Tamburlaine, Part I*, or *Dr Faustus*. In its conception, it looks forward to *Dr Faustus*, rather than backwards to *Part I*, though it makes, of course, continual reference to the first part and shows indeed many ironic contrasts with it.

The theme of the first part of *Tamburlaine* is the power and splend-our of the human will, which bears down all opposition and by its own native force achieves its desires. Tamburlaine is shown to us in the double rôle of warrior and lover. In both he is irresistible and the play reaches its climax in his conquest of Zenocrate's father, the Soldan, and the crowning of Zenocrate as Queen and Empress of the kingdoms he has conquered. The structure of the play is extremely simple and could be plotted as a single rising line on a graph; there are no setbacks. The world into which Tamburlaine, the unknown Scythian shepherd, bursts like a kind of portent is decadent, divided and torn by petty strife. Little dignity or grandeur is given to his opponents and, as Miss Ellis-Fermor justly remarks, the tragic pity, voiced by Zenocrate, for 'the Turk and his great empress' is allowed only slight scope. Opposition appears to melt away at Tamburlaine's mere appearance. Theridamas, sent with an army against him, is won over by his pre-sence and comes over to his side without a battle; Cosroe, who de-thrones his brother and plans to use Tamburlaine for his own purposes, is easily overthrown. In love the path is equally straight. Zenocrate, betrothed to the Prince of Arabia, when captured by Tamburlaine, makes no defiance. We are not even shown a wooing; at their second meeting, she is already in love with him and yields without a show of resistance, seeming to range herself on his side, as the others do, by instinct.

The theme of the second part is very different. Man's desires and aspirations may be limitless, but their fulfilment is limited by forces outside the control of the will. There are certain facts, of which death is the most obvious, which no aspiration and no force of soul can conquer. There is a sort of stubbornness in the stuff of experience which frustrates and resists the human will. The world is not the plaything of the ambitious mind. There are even hints in the play that there is an order in the world, of which men's minds are a part, and that man acts against this order at his peril. This theme of the clash between man's desires and his experience demands a more complex structure for its expression than was demanded by the theme of the triumphant human will in the first part. If the first part can be plotted as a steadily rising line, the second can be thought of as two lines, the line of Tamburlaine and that of his enemies. Neither rises or falls steadily, but on the whole it can be said that the forces opposing Tamburlaine grow in strength during the first half of the play and reach their zenith in the third act, and that after this we see the power of Tamburlaine reasserting itself, until, at the moment of his greatest triumph, he is struck down by death. But a graph of two lines does not really express the play's structure, since it leaves unrepresented the force that in the end destroys the hero. This force (it can be called Necessity or God, according to one's interpretation of Marlowe's religious thought) appears from time to time in the body of the play and in the end reduces the contest between Tamburlaine and his foes to an episode in the world's pattern; it provides a kind of ground swell to the whole play. The truth of this analysis can only be brought out by a detailed examination of the plot.

The second part, like the first, does not open with the hero, but with his opponents; but, whereas in the first part they are shown as despicable, in the second they are dignified and worthy of respect. At the beginning of the first part we saw the kingdom of Persia fallen into the hands of a fool, whose brother was plotting with the aid of a faction at the court to dethrone him. In the second part we find the Turkish kings deciding upon a truce with the Christians, in order to secure their rear against attack while they fight with Tamburlaine. That is to say, the first part showed us a world of disunity and strife, which fell an easy prey to Tamburlaine's ambition, while the second shows us a world aware of the menace of Tamburlaine and organizing itself to oppose him. By the second scene of the first act the truce has been made and Orcanes with his allies is prepared for Tamburlaine's attack. In the third scene we meet Callapine, the captive son of Bajazeth, who, by promises and bribes, wins over his gaoler, Almeda, to betray his trust and assist in an escape. This scene, in which a servant of Tamburlaine's is won over from him by the lure of money and glory, would be inconceivable in the first part. There all the attraction and the lures are on Tamburlaine's side; he is a kind of magnet, attracting the ambitious towards him. The treachery of his servant at the opening of the second part suggests that we have no longer to do with the conquering demi-god of the first part; the Tamburlaine spell is not working. In the next scene Tamburlaine himself appears and the same feeling is just hinted at. For all his power of will, he is unable to mould his sons as he pleases. He is distressed by their unwarlike appearance, satisfied by the bloodthirsty remarks of two of them, but baffled by the unabashed cowardice of Calyphas. Miss Ellis-Fermor's notes to this scene speak of 'that hint of frustration and anxiety which grows more definite as this part of the play progresses'. But both the scene of Callapine's escape and that of

Calyphas's unnatural pacificism give only hints and the old Tamburlaine soon reasserts himself. His companions, Theridamas, Techelles and Usumcasane, enter with news of conquering campaigns and of great armies come to fight on his side. The first act ends with Tamburlaine apparently all-powerful, banqueting in triumph among his subject kings.

The second act opens with a setback for the enemies of Tamburlaine. The Christian kings decide to break their truce with the Turks, on the ground that faith need not be kept with infidels. When the news of this treachery is brought to Orcanes, he, an unbeliever, makes the famous appeal to the Christ whom the Christians worship, to show his Godhead by punishing the perjury of his servants. Marlowe could not resist the opportunity of underlining the contrast between the faith of Christians and their works, but the real meaning of the episode lies in the lines in which Marlowe, through the mouth of Orcanes, expresses his belief that the God who 'everywhere fills every continent with strange infusion of his sacred vigour' is a God of purity as well as of power, and that he punishes the sins of men. Orcanes's appeal to Christ is answered; the Christians flee in discomfiture, acknowledging their fate is just. The opponents of Tamburlaine, weakened at the beginning of the act, end in a stronger position through having surmounted the trial, and the whole moral feeling of the episode tells against the arrogance of Tamburlaine. The action passes at once and without warning to the deathbed of Zenocrate and here the moral is too clear to need any pointing; it is given with sad brevity by the watching Theridamas:

> Ah, good my lord, be patient! she is dead,
> And all this raging cannot make her live.

The third act opens with a scene which is obviously intended to parallel Act 1, scene 6. There, Tamburlaine, having summoned his subject kings, assessed his forces for the coming campaign: here, Callapine, having been crowned with his father's crown Emperor of Turkey, is told by his tributary kings what strength they can bring for the coming struggle with Tamburlaine. This scene shows Callapine at the peak of his power; the confederation against Tamburlaine is at its height. By contrast, Tamburlaine in the next scene is at his most dejected, celebrating the death of Zenocrate by the futile and savage burning of a town. Having lost his wife, he turns to his sons for consolation, only to find himself baffled by the weakness of Calyphas. His attention is distracted by the other two, who show a dutiful indifference to pain, but a hint is given here of another of those forces which hamper us in the execution of our ambitions, the resistance of other wills, which refuse to accept the parts we assign to them.

This theme is developed in a subsidiary episode, which has usually been regarded as mere padding, that of Theridamas and Olympia, the

Captain's wife. In reading this episode, one recalls the parallel situation of the first part, when Zenocrate, captured as a prize of war, also charms her conqueror by her beauty. There the conqueror was as successful in love as in war and his captive responded to his passion before he spoke of it. Theridamas, the hero of this episode, is associated in our minds with Tamburlaine, as his closest friend and most loyal follower; his fortunes have followed those of his master. The rebuff he suffers here at the hands of Olympia, who prefers death to his love, and eludes him finally, when he seems to have absolute power over her, by a clever ruse, seems to reflect back on Tamburlaine himself.

The death of Olympia follows immediately upon the murder of Calyphas, which is itself an example of failure coming on the heels of success. Act 3 ends with a scolding match between Tamburlaine and the Turkish kings and in Act 4, scene 1 Tamburlaine wins his first great victory over Orcanes and his allies; but the moment of triumph is spoilt by the cowardice of Calyphas and he celebrates his victory by the murder of his son, whom he can kill, but cannot force to obey him. It is possible that Marlowe had some sympathy with the effeminate Calyphas (he certainly provides him with some good ironic comment on his father); but one must be careful not to read a modern criticism of the value of military exploits into what may have seemed to the Elizabethans obvious wrong-headedness, nor must one overestimate the value of the silence with which he dies. Nevertheless, it is worth noting that though the bystanders plead for his life, Calyphas himself says nothing. This may be a deliberate touch, the last defiance of the weakling, or it may be that Marlowe forgot the victim in his interest in the executioner; or, perhaps, his father's reference to his 'fainting soul' is to be taken literally. But the whole treatment of Calyphas suggests something more subtle than the traditional coward; his distaste for war and his refusal to find his father impressive are positive rather than negative attitudes, and his silent death may be due partly to his realization of his father's implacability and partly to his desire to infuriate him by not cowering. In the general development of the play, the two episodes of Olympia and Calyphas taken together prepare us for the dénouement; they both show the limitations of human power, here thwarted by other human wills. Occurring as they do, at the moment of Tamburlaine's first military success in this play, they hint at the hollowness of such triumphs; and, in this context, the mad bombast of Tamburlaine, which, in the last scene of the fourth act, culminates in the yoking of the conquered kings to his chariot, is seen for what it is: an impious assertion of human pride, ludicrous in its excess, and by its exaggeration revealing the palpable falseness of his claim to absolute power.

Throughout the fifth act the power of Tamburlaine grows and that of his foes declines. The Governor of Babylon makes a show of resistance, but yields to pressure: the conquered kings have a moment of revolt, but are soon 'bridled'. Tamburlaine, defying Mahomet, and with him conventional religious observances, claims that he is the great servant and instrument of the only true God.

> There is a God, full of revenging wrath,
> From whom the thunder and the lightning breaks,
> Whose scourge I am, and him will I obey.

It is at the height of his power that Tamburlaine is struck down. Even when dying he can, by his mere presence, put the army of Callapine to flight; but his last and greatest victory is only the prelude to death. Through the last half of the play, as his power has grown, so have the warnings of fate, mere hints in the first act, grown louder. Now sickness proves him a man who 'was termed the terror of the world'. In words gentler and graver than one would expect, and which are often overlooked, Tamburlaine, in his dying admonition to his heir, himself moralizes his end:

> Nor bar thy mind that magnanimity
> That nobly must admit necessity.

It is by necessity that 'Tamburlaine the scourge of God must die'.

It cannot be claimed that the execution of *Tamburlaine, Part 2* is equal to the conception, but the play contains less irrelevance than is usually imagined, and it is an interesting early attempt at a more complicated tragic pattern than the first part or *Dr Faustus* can show. . . .

The basis of the pattern in *Tamburlaine, Part 2* is the struggle of Tamburlaine and Callapine; but into this conflict of military and political power is woven the theme of necessity, a necessity which Marlowe tries to moralize. It is moralized early in the play by the answer which the prayer of the good heathen Orcanes receives, and, in the later half, by the mad pride of Tamburlaine, which gives his death the quality of a punishment. The first part of *Tamburlaine* glorifies the human will: the second displays its inevitable limits. It is a first handling of the theme of *Dr Faustus*—a weaker handling, because Tamburlaine's ambitions are cruder than those of Faustus, and because there is little feeling in *Tamburlaine, Part 2* for the paradoxes that make up the tragedy of the later play. Faustus, aiming at being more than man, becomes less, for he cuts himself off from the common mercies of God; desiring all knowledge, he finds the great secret barred from him, for he may learn nothing 'that is against our kingdom'; desiring all power, he finds himself the slave of Mephistophilis, who, he had thought, was to be his servant. *Dr Faustus*, in spite of its mutilated state, expresses clearly the great tragic idea of the essential vanity of desires which refuse to take into account the limitations of humanity. The theme of *Tamburlaine, Part 2* is less profoundly tragic than this, and Marlowe shows little sense that the goods which Tamburlaine pursues are in the end themselves unsatisfying. The play proclaims only the idea of necessity, which the magnanimous mind must 'nobly admit', and its moral is the simple medieval one of the inevitability of death. But the arrival of that final check to Tamburlaine's fantasies of omnipotence is more carefully prepared for than is usually admitted and the earlier episodes of the play, sometimes judged to be mere padding, are mainly anticipations of the final catastrophe and variations on the underlying theme.

From 'The Second Part of *Tamburlaine the Great*', in *Modern Language Review*, vol. XXXVII, 1942, pp. 18–24.

M. M. MAHOOD

The Jew of Malta:
A Contracted World

... *The Jew of Malta* is a tragic farce,[1] at once both terrifying and absurd. The world it exhibits, by its wide dissimilarity to life as we know it, is ludicrous beyond the bounds of comedy; yet it frightens by reason of a certain logical relationship with reality. If certain conditions governed the world as we know it, it would be exactly like the Malta ruled by Ferneze and terrorized by the Jew Barabas. Chief among these conditions would be the conviction, acknowledged or concealed, of all such a world's inhabitants, that the material order comprised the whole of existence. Throughout his first two tragedies, Marlowe never lets us forget the existence of worlds other than the visible—the Heaven which Tamburlaine's pride impels him to defy, the Hell into which Faustus is plunged by his despair. In *The Jew of Malta* there is no such impingement of one order of being upon another. The play depicts a world which has cut itself off entirely from the transcendent. The God invoked by Barabas is a 'Prime Motor', who has set the machine in motion and left it to run as best it may. There is no possibility here of intervention by the Divine Justice that pursues Tamburlaine or by the Divine Mercy offered to Faustus.

Such contraction of the drama's scope to mundane, social matter, almost unparalleled in tragedy, imparts a feeling of constriction to the opening scene. Tamburlaine and Faustus are both physically and mentally restless; the one marches over great areas of the eastern hemisphere, the other, 'to prooue *Cosmography*', moves invisible over the length and breadth of Europe. [All quotations are from C. F. T. Brooke's edition of Marlowe's *Works*, 1910.] In contrast, *The Jew of Malta* has for its setting an island of the land-locked Mediterranean; and Barabas is content to remain in his counting-house where the wealth of many lands is compressed into the 'little room' of his jewels. By comparison with Marlowe's earlier plays, *The Jew of Malta* shows an impoverishment in the character of the hero, as well as in the play's setting. Where Tamburlaine and Faustus sought to control, the one by conquest and the other by knowledge, Barabas is satisfied to plunder:

[1] T. S. Eliot, *Elizabethan Essays*, p. 28.

> What more may Heauen doe for earthly man
> Then thus to powre out plenty in their laps,
> Ripping the bowls of the earth for them,
> Making the Sea their seruant, and the winds
> To driue their substance with successefull blasts?   145–9

The Jew turns his back upon the coloured splendours of his Mediterranean world, content with the reflection of fire and sea and sky in the precious stones which comprise his wealth. If any of an artist's delight in form and hue remains in Barabas's praise of his treasure, it has been contaminated by the worldly sense of values which is inimical to art. And although he holds a king's ransom in his hand when the play opens, Barabas is soon forced to admit that he has no hope of a crown; no principality awaits this Machiavellian. Thus in comparison with Tamburlaine and Faustus, the Jew appears a shrunken figure, withered in body and mind. The earlier heroes try to embody, in Zenocrate and Helen, their scarcely attainable ideal of love's perfection. For Barabas there remains only the memory of old lust, recalled in lines of flat indifference:

> *Friar.*   Thou has committed—
> *Barabas.* Fornication? but that was in another Country:
>   And besides, the Wench is dead.   1549–51

Tamburlaine's aspirations and Faustus's fears impart a sense of the transcendental to the earlier tragedies; and because their deaths reveal certain truths about this immaterial world, they are made the occasions of great poetry. Barabas never makes any discovery of this kind. He is merely exterminated, and Marlowe does not waste good verse on his ending.

The ruling philosophy of this constricted and materialist world is 'each man for himself and the devil take the hindmost'. In the Jew's monstrous egotism, this philosophy is carried to its logical extreme. Barabas is prepared to sacrifice his one natural affection, his love for his daughter Abigail, to his principle—if anything so unprincipled deserves the name—of *'Ego mihimet sum semper proximus'* (l. 228). Natural affections, he instructs his slave Ithamore, are mere encumbrances in such a society:

> First be thou voyd of these affections,
> Compassion, loue, vaine hope, and hartlesse feare,
> Be mou'd at nothing, see thou pitty none.   934–6

This cynical opportunism was accredited by the Elizabethans to Machiavelli, whose philosophy they knew chiefly through the adverse comments of Gentillet and others.[2] The Prologue of Marlowe's play is spoken by 'The Ghost of Machivel', who claims the Jew for his disciple. Such pronouncements as:

[2] R. Battenhouse, *Marlowe's 'Tamburlaine'*, pp. 41–9.

in extremitie
We ought to make barre of no policie,   507–8

and

And since by wrong thou got'st Authority,
Maintaine it brauely by firme policy   2136–7

identify Barabas as a Machiavellian, since a 'politician', on the Elizabethan stage, was always an admirer of Machiavelli's opportunist
doctrines. Allusions to the Borgias and other Italian poisoners add to
an atmosphere of transalpine villainy calculated to send a shiver down
every English Protestant spine.

The Jew is not, however, the only villain in the piece. In a world
where love, justice, honesty have all lost their validity, no character
is fundamentally better than the frankly opportunist Barabas. The
Christians among whom he lives have long since diverted their worship from God to Mammon. Practices and phrases which once were
the expression of spiritual experiences linger amongst them as 'ideals'
in the Shavian sense—truths which are outworn from a materialist
viewpoint, but which are retained for the commercial value of their
respectability. Commercial values are, indeed, the only standards of
the society which Marlowe has imagined in *The Jew of Malta*. 'What
wind drives you thus into *Malta* rhode?' Ferneze asks the Basso; and
the Turk's reply sets the mood for the whole play:

The wind that bloweth all the world besides,
Desire of gold.   1422–3

Time and again Barabas is able to excuse his actions on the grounds
that the Christians, for all their pretended horror of usury, are just
as rapacious as he:

Thus louing neither, will I liue with both,
Making a profit of my policie;
And he from whom my most aduantage comes,
Shall be my friend.
This is the life we Iewes are vs'd to lead;
And reason too, for Christians doe the like.   2213–18

He prepares for one of his crimes with the words: 'Now will I shew
my selfe to haue more of the Serpent Then the Doue; that is, more
knaue than foole' (ll. 797–8). Since the world of *The Jew of Malta* is
one into which ethical considerations do not enter, intelligence alone
counts. Characters are not good or bad; they have fewer or more wits
about them. As in Jonsonian comedy, the rogue who deceives every-
body except himself is far more acceptable than the self-deceiving
hypocrite who flatters himself that his own shady deeds are directed
by the highest motives. Or, as Barabas puts it,

> A counterfet profession is better
> Then vnseene hypocrisie.   531–2

This contrast of self-confessed opportunism with self-concealed greed is most marked in the scene between Ferneze and Barabas, in which the Governor deprives the Jew of all his possessions in order to obtain tribute money for the Turks. When the Jew asks if he and his fellow-Jews are to contribute 'equally' with the Maltese, Ferneze replies in words which are both unctuous with hypocrisy and fierce with superstitious hatred:

> No, Iew, like infidels.
> For through our sufferance of your hatefull liues,
> Who stand accursed in the sight of heauen,
> These taxes and afflictions are befal'ne.   294–7

To this the First Knight self-righteously adds:

> If your first curse fall heauy on thy head,
> And make thee poore and scornd of all the world,
> 'Tis not our fault, but thy inherent sinne.   340–2

There is no doubting Marlowe's ironic intention in the Governor's next speech:

> Excesse of wealth is cause of couetousnesse:
> And couetousnesse, oh 'tis a monstrous sinne.   355–7

Again, Ferneze's use of the word 'profession' in

> No, *Barabas*, to staine our hands with blood
> Is farre from vs and our profession,   377–8

recalls the 'profession' of the Puritans, whose hypocrisy was so often the butt of Elizabethan stage satire. Barabas several times uses the word in his contemptuous allusions to the Christians. Through such subtle direction of their feelings, the audience are driven to sympathize with Barabas; and when Ferneze, having despoiled the Jew of all his possessions, adds insult to injury by saying, in sanctimonious tones,

> Content thee, *Barabas*, thou hast nought but right,

the audience must feel itself compelled to applaud Barabas's retort:

> Your extreme right does me exceeding wrong.   385–6

Ferneze's dealings with the Turks display the same hypocrisy. As in the Sigismund scenes of *Tamburlaine* (Part II), Marlowe made use of the current notion that a promise made to a heretic need not be kept, to expose the double-dealing of those who thus justified their treachery on religious grounds. At del Bosco's persuasion, Ferneze breaks his undertaking to pay the Turkish tribute (presumably he retains for his own treasury the money which he has exacted from

Barabas), and justifies his action with some high-sounding phrases about honour (l. 791). Barabas supplies the obvious comment that if Christians thus deceive those who are not of their own faith, a Jew has as good a pretext for cheating a Gentile:

> It's no sinne to deceiue a Christian;
> For they themselues hold it a principle,
> Faith is not to be held with Heretickes;
> But all are Hereticks that are not Iewes.   1074–7

The acquisitive passion directs not only all the actions of Ferneze and his court, but also those of the other groups of characters. There is nothing to commend the predatory gallants, Lodowick and Mathias; the tone for their wooing of the Jew's daughter is set by the scenes between Lodowick and Barabas in which Abigail is alluded to, in a series of innuendoes, as a diamond which Lodowick wishes to buy. Abigail herself is the one character in the play who is not ruled by greed, and her conversion represents an attempt to break free from the limitations of the narrow, materialistic society which surrounds her. The attempt is rendered pathetic by the fact that the religious, amongst whom she hopes to find release, are as mercenary as the outside world which they pretend to shun. Barabas's sneer,

> And yet I know the prayers of those Nuns
> And holy Fryers, hauing mony for their paines
> Are wondrous; *and indeed doe no man good*   843–5

is substantiated by the behaviour of the 'two religious Caterpillers', the friars of rival orders who come to blows over Barabas's announcement that he will enter into religion and bestow his fortune on the monastery of his choice. Lastly, the 'low-life' group of characters— Ithamore, Pilia-Borza and the Courtesan—are shown, in their blackmailing of the Jew, to be as rapacious as the rest. Turk, Moor, Christian and Jew are all as bad as each other, and in these circumstances a cynical 'policy' is to be preferred to a hypocritical 'profession' which cloaks greed in a false devotion:

> Rather had I a Iew be hated thus,
> Then pittied in a Christian pouerty:
> For I can see no fruits in all their faith,
> But malice, falshood, and excessiue pride,
> Which me thinkes fits not their profession.   152–6

There is something strangely prophetic of the mercantile society of later times in this Mammon-worshipping world of Marlowe's invention. Barabas has much of the sardonic clear-sightedness of those who have made it their work to reveal the sham values of such a society. Were the same theme to be treated by a twentieth-century dramatist, Barabas might be shown as a kind of Undershaft, exposing the low motives behind the high-sounding phrases of those around him, and the curtain would come down upon Ferneze in the cauldron. But shrewd and sensitive as was Marlowe's grasp of the humanist problem, he was no prophet of a future society; and even while he felt the Machiavellian realist to be superior to his hypocritically idealist victims, he understood the impoverishment entailed by Barabas's materialistic outlook. Humanism progressed backward. Barabas's cynicism lacks the tragic dignity of Tamburlaine's aspiration or of Faustus's despair; and by the end of the play the Jew has become a monster and not even a sinister monster.

Barabas is a diminished figure, but he is still a vital one. Life may be limited for him to a single plane of existence; nevertheless, he finds the tooth-and-claw struggle for wealth highly enjoyable. Deprived of all he held dear, he can still say, 'No, I will liue; nor loath I this my life' (l. 501). But in Marlowe's *Edward II,* the final stage of the humanist's self-destruction is portrayed: the denial, not only of human spirituality and greatness, but of life itself. . . .

From 'Marlowe's Heroes', in *Poetry and Humanism*, Kennikat Press, Inc., Port Washington, N.Y., 1967, pp. 54–86 (74–81).

HARRY LEVIN

The Jew of Malta:
Poor Old Rich Man

... Marlowe was never more the devil's advocate than when he chose
a wandering Jew for his hero. His working model was less a human
being than a bugbear of folklore, inasmuch as the Jews were officially
banished from England between the reign of Edward I and the protec-
torate of Oliver Cromwell. In certain regions of the Mediterranean,
Jewish financiers and politicians had risen to power in the sixteenth
century; and Marlowe, whose play has no literary source, must have
come across anecdotes about them. In his selection of a name there is
a deeper significance, for Barabas was the criminal whom the Jews
preferred to Jesus, when Pilate offered to release a prisoner. One of
the witnesses against Marlowe's atheism, Richard Baines, quotes his
assertion: 'That Crist deserved better to dy then Barrabas and that
the Jewes made a good Choise, though Barrabas were both a thief
and a murtherer'. It could also be said that, if Christ died for all men,
he died most immediately for Barabas; and that Barabas was the man
whose mundane existence profited most immediately from Christ's
sacrifice. From the perspective of historical criticism, Barabas actually
seems to have been an insurrectionist. Marlowe, in instinctively taking
his side, identifies his Jew with the Antichrist. Hence the crude cartoon
becomes an apocalyptic monstrosity, whose temporal kingdom is the
earth itself. It is no idle jest when Ithamore remarks of Barabas: 'The
Hat he weares, *Iudas* left vnder the Elder when he hang'd himselfe'
(1988) [Quotations from *The Jew of Malta* are from C. F. T. Brooke's
edition of Marlowe's *Works*, 1910]. When Alleyn wore it with the
accustomed gabardine, the red beard, and the hyperbolic nose, he must
have seemed the exemplification of guile, acquisitiveness, and treachery. . . .

The starting point of the play is the exit of Machiavel, who pulls
back the arras that curtains the inner stage and thereby discovers
Barabas in his counting-house. We are not asked to believe that this
shallow recess is anything more than concretely strikes the eye. This
is a back-room, not the façade of a palace. True, the stage direction
indicates heaps of coins; but we are less impressed by them than by
Barabas's gesture of dismissal.

Fye; what a trouble tis to count this trash.   42

We are dazzled, not because riches are dangled before us, but because they are tossed aside; because precious stones are handled 'like pibble-stones' (58). Not that Barabas is indifferent to them; soon enough he makes it evident that gold is to him what the crown is to Tamburlaine, 'felicity' (689); and he completes that blasphemy by marking his buried treasure with the sign of the cross. But it vastly increases the scale of his affluence to reckon it up so dryly and casually. Barabas out-Herods Tamburlaine by making hyperboles sound like understatements; he values the least of his jewels at a king's ransom. His will to power is gratified less by possession than by control. In this he does not resemble the conqueror so much as he adumbrates the capitalist; and Marlowe has grasped what is truly imaginative, what in his time was almost heroic, about business enterprise. To audit bills of lading for Indian argosies, to project empires by double-entry book-keeping, to enthrone and dethrone royalties by loans—that is indeed 'a kingly kinde of trade' (2330). In the succinct formulations of Barabas,

> Infinite riches in a little roome,   72

Marlowe sublimates his expansive ideal from the plane of economics to that of aesthetics. The line itself is perfect in its symmetry; each half begins with the syllable 'in' and proceeds through antithetical adjectives to alliterative nouns; six of the ten vowels are short *i*'s; and nothing could be more Marlovian than the underlying notion of containing the uncontainable. It is hard to imagine how a larger amount of implication could be more compactly ordered within a single pentameter. Ruskin once categorically declared that a miser could not sing about his gold; James Russell Lowell, on the contrary, has described this line as 'the very poetry of avarice'; and if that be a contradiction in terms, it matches the contradictions of Marlowe's theme. . . .

Barabas's policy spins a plot for *The Jew of Malta* which can be pursued on three interconnecting levels. The conventions of English drama prescribed an underplot, which is ordinarily a burlesque of the main plot; clowns are cast as servants and play the zany to their respective masters; and the stolen sheep is a symbolic counterpart of the infant Jesus in the *Second Shepherds' Play* of Wakefield. With the full development of tragedy, there is a similar ramification upwards, which might conveniently be called the overplot. That is the stuff of history as it impinges upon the more personal concerns of the characters; thus the events of *The Spanish Tragedy* are precipitated by wars between Spain and Portugal. Thus, with *Hamlet*, the overplot is conditioned by the dynastic relations of Denmark and Norway and Poland; while the main plot concentrates upon Hamlet's revenge against Claudius; and the underplot—which, in this instance, is more romantic than comic—has to do with the household of Polonius, and most particularly with Ophelia. *The Jew of Malta* is similarly constructed, and probably helped to fix this triple method of construction. The overplot, framed by the siege, is the inter-relationship between the Christians and Jews, the Spaniards and Turks. It is connected with the main plot through the peculations of Barabas, who is caught up in the underplot through his misplaced confidence in Ithamore. The bonds of self-interest connect the central intrigue, which involves usury, with power politics upon the upper level and with blackmail upon the lower. Blackmail is the tax that Barabas pays on his ill-gotten hoards; but his rear-guard actions against the blackmailers are more successful than his efforts to beat the politicians at their own game.

Morally, all of them operate on the same level, and that is precisely what Marlowe is pointing out. In order to sell a cargo of Turkish slaves, the Spanish Vice-Admiral talks the Governor into breaking the treaty between Malta and the Turks. It is not merely in the slave market, but in the counting-house and the senate chamber, that men are bought and sold. As for the traffic in women, Ithamore becomes ensnared in it; soon after Barabas buys him, he falls into the hands of the courtesan Bellamira and her bullying companion, Pilia-Borza—whose name, meaning 'pick-purse', denotes the least sinister of his activities. The confidence game that this nefarious couple practises on Barabas, through their hold over Ithamore, was known in the Elizabethan underworld as 'cross-biting'. By whatever name it goes, it reduces eroticism to chicanery; it debases Marlowe's *libido sentiendi* to its most ignoble manifestation. Ithamore addresses Bellamira as if she were Zenocrate or Helen of Troy, instead of a woman whose professional habit is to do the persuading on her own behalf. The invitation to love, as he extends it, is sweetened for vulgar tastes; the classical meadows of Epicureanism now 'beare Sugar Canes'; and rhetorical enticements sink into bathos with a couplet which burlesques 'The Passionate Shepherd':

> Thou in those Groues, by *Dis* aboue,
> Shalt liue with me and be my loue.   1815–6

The principle of double-dealing, which prevails on all sides in Malta, is established in the scene where the Governor summons the Jews to raise funds for the Turkish tribute. Distinguishing somewhat pharisaically between his profession and theirs, he offers the alternative of conversion, which none of them accepts. When he mulcts them of half their estates, the other Jews comply at once; and since Barabas refuses, his wealth is entirely confiscated. To him, therefore, his co-religionists are Job's comforters; yet, from the outset, his devotion has centred less on his race than on his selfish interests. He finds a justification in observing that Christians preach religion and practise opportunism.

> What? bring you Scripture to confirm your wrongs?
> Preach me not out of my possessions.   343–4

From one of the Knights, he picks up the catchword that seems to explain the disparity between what they profess and what they really do:

> I, policie? that's their profession.   393

In endeavouring to recover his lost fortune, he resolves to 'make barre of no policie' (508). He justifies his next stratagem on the grounds that 'a counterfet profession' (531), his daughter's pretended conversion, is better than 'vnseene hypocrisie', than the unexposed perfidies of professed believers. He admonishes his daughter that religion

> Hides many mischiefes from suspition.   520

His cynicism seems altogether justified when the Knights break a double faith, refusing to pay the Turks the money they have seized for that purpose from Barabas. Their argument, the one that the Christians used in *Tamburlaine* when they violated their oath to their Mohammedan allies, proves a useful rationalization for Barabas:

> It's no sinne to deciue a Christian;
> For they themselues hold it a principle,
> Faith is not to be held with Heretickes;
> But all are Hereticks that are not Iewes.   1074–7

Ithamore, going over to the other side, can quote this dangerous scripture against his master:

> To vndoe a Iew is a charity, and not sinne.   2001

After the Christians have broken their league with the Turks, Barabas leagues with the Turks against the Knights. His fatal mistake is to betray his new allies to his old enemies, the Christians, by whom he thereupon is promptly betrayed. He is repaid in kind; but his Turkish victims have been comparatively honourable; and he ends as an inadvertent defender of Christendom. Meanwhile, by craftily pitting infidels against believers, one belief against another, fanaticism against Atheism, Marlowe has dramatized the dialectics of comparative religion.

Is there, then, no such thing as sincere devotion? Perhaps some unfortunate person, Barabas is willing to allow,

> Happily some haplesse man hath conscience.   157

If so, he does not appear on the Maltese horizon. But by chance, by that ironic destiny which Thomas Hardy calls 'hap', there is one woman,

> one sole Daughter, whom I hold as deare
> As *Agamemnon* did his *Iphigen*.   175–6

Though Agamemnon is less relevant than Jephtha might have been, the simile is an omen for Abigall, the single disinterested character in the play, who is characterized by the first four words she speaks: 'Not for my selfe . . .' (462). Her father lovingly repeats her name, as David repeated the name of Absalom. His policy dictates her profession, when in filial duty she re-enters his former house, which has been converted into a nunnery. When she recognizes that she has been the unwitting instrument of his revenge, 'experience, purchased with griefe', opens her eyes to 'the difference of things' (1285). She now experiences a genuine vocation, perceiving that

> there is no loue on earth,
> Pitty in Iewes, nor piety in Turkes.   1270–1

By taking the veil, she extinguishes the latent spark of tenderness in Barabas, who retaliates by poisoning all the nuns. Stricken, she has the moral satisfaction of confessing that she dies a Christian. But the pathos of these last words is undercut by the cynical dictum of her confessor:

> I, and a Virgin too, that grieues me most.   1497

Abigall's honesty, in the Elizabethan sense of chastity as well as sincerity, is confirmed by her death; but she finds no sanctuary among the religious. Her innocent lover, Don Mathias, has been slain while slaying the Governor's son, Don Lodowick, in a duel contrived by the vengeful Barabas. This contrivance gives a Marlovian twist to one of the strangest obsessions of the European consciousness, the legend of the Jew's daughter, who serves as a decoy in luring a Christian youth to his doom by her father's knife in their dark habitation. . . .

Barabas invokes the birds of the air, the raven before and the lark after Abigall has aided him to regain his moneybags. The night scene, in its imagery and staging, curiously foreshadows the balcony scene in *Romeo and Juliet*. When Abigall—who, like Juliet, is 'scarce 14 yeares of age' (621)—appears on the upper stage, Barabas exclaims:

> But stay, what starre shines yonder in the *East*?
> The Loadstarre of my life, if *Abigall*.   680–1

When Shakespeare copies this picture, he brightens it, in accordance with the more youthful and ardent mood of Romeo:

> But soft, what light through yonder window breaks?
> It is the East, and *Iuliet* is the Sunne.   II, ii, 2–3

There is another moment which looks ahead to Shakespeare's romantic tragedy; and that comes after the duel, when the Governor eulogizes the rival lovers and promises to bury them in the same monument. If this midpoint had been the ending, the drama might have retained its equilibrium; there would have been enough grievances and sufferings on both sides. With the disappearance of the fragile heroine and of the lyrical touches that cluster about her, tragedy is overshadowed by revenge. But we might have realized, when Abigall introduced herself to the Abbess as

> The hopelesse daughter of a haplesse Iew,   557

that Marlowe was shaping his play by the sterner conventions of *The Spanish Tragedy* and Kyd's Hieronimo,

> The hopeless father of a hapless Sonne.   IV, iv, 84

Between revenge and romance, between tragedy and comedy, *The Merchant of Venice* provides a Shakespearian compromise. It gives the benediction of a happy ending to the legend of the Jew's daughter; and it allows the Jewish protagonist, for better or for worse, his day in court. Legalism both narrows and humanizes Shylock, in contradistinction to Barabas, who for the most part lives outside the law and does not clamour for it until it has overtaken him. In rounding off the angles and mitigating the harshness of Marlowe's caricature, Shakespeare loses something of its intensity. The mixed emotions of Shylock, wailing, 'O my ducats, O my daughter' (II, viii, 15), are muted by being reported at second hand. We see and hear, we recall and recoil from the unholy joy of Barabas:

> Oh girle, oh gold, oh beauty, oh my blisse!   695

If the comparison is not with Shakespeare but with Marlowe's earlier writing, *The Jew of Malta* registers enormous gains in flexibility. Except when Barabas mutters to himself in a *lingua franca* of Spanish and Italian, the diction is plainer and much saltier. The average length of an individual speech is no more than 2.8 lines, as differentiated from the second part of *Tamburlaine,* where it runs to 6.3. This implies, theatrically speaking, more than twice as many cues in the later play, with a consequent thickening of the dialogue and a general quickening of the action. It follows that there are fewer monologues, although Barabas delivers a number of them—in that Biblical vein which transforms the basic modes of Tamburlaine's rhetoric, the threat and the plea, into the curse, the jeremiad, the prophecy. The Prophets had spoken English blank verse in Greene and Lodge's *Looking-Glass for London,* as had the Psalmist in Peele's *David and Bethsabe.* But *The Jew of Malta* requires some means of private comment, as well as public speech, to express the cross-purposes between policy and profession, deeds and words. It leans much more upon the soliloquy, which the extroverted Tamburlaine hardly needed, and its characteristic mode is the aside. Marlowe did not invent this simplistic device; actors had voiced their thoughts to audiences before they had exchanged them with each other; and characterization of the villain was, for obvious reasons, peculiarly dependent upon that convention. It could not be disregarded by a playwright who had to guide introverted

characters through the Machiavellian province of false declarations
and unvoiced intentions. '*I must dissemble,*' says Barabas (1556), and
the italics alert the reader to what the spectator feels when the spoken
words are aimed at him in a stage whisper. The actor is professionally
a dissembler, etymologically a hypocrite. The histrionics of Barabas
are not confined to his role in the disguise of a French musician. Except
for his unwarranted confidences to his daughter and to his slave, he
is always acting, always disguised. We, who overhear his asides and
soliloquies, are his only trustworthy confidants. We are therefore in
collusion with Barabas. We revel in his malice, we share his guilt.
We are the 'worldlings' to whom he addresses himself (2332).

This understanding is the framework of Marlowe's irony. When
Barabas is first interrogated by the Knights, his replies are deliberately
naïve; we know that he knows what they want from him; but he
dissembles his shrewdness, plays the *Eiron,* and fences with the
Governor. Often he utters no more than a line at a time, and engages
in stichomythy—in capping line for line—with his interlocutors.
Repartee is facilitated by Marlowe's increasing willingness to break off
a speech and start upon another at the caesura, without interrupting
the rhythm of the blank verse. Speeches of less than a line are still
rather tentative, and prose is a more favourable climate than verse for
the cultivation of pithy dialogue. Possibly the most striking advance
beyond *Tamburlaine* is the transition from a voluble to a laconic style,
from Ciceronian periods to Senecan aphorisms. Effects depend, not
upon saying everything, but upon keeping certain things unsaid. The
climax of ironic dissimulation comes with the scene where the two
Friars 'exclaime against' Barabas (1502). In their association with the
nuns, Marlowe has lost no opportunity for anticlerical innuendo; now
the 'two religious Caterpillers' hold the upper hand over Barabas, since
they have learned of his crimes from the dying Abigall; but since they
are bound by the seal of confession, they cannot lodge a downright
accusation. He has both these considerations in mind, as do we, when
he parries their hesitating denunciations.

> Thou art a—,   1539

says one Friar; and Barabas admits what is common knowledge, that
he is a Jew and a usurer.

> Thou hast committed—,   1549

says the other, and again the admission is an evasion:

> Fornication? but that was in another Country:
> And besides, the Wench is dead.   1550-1

For anyone else there might be, for others there have been, romance
and even tragedy in the reminiscence. For Barabas it is simply an alibi,
a statute of limitations. He is content to remind the Friars, with a

legalistic shrug, that the Seventh Commandment is not to be taken as
seriously as the Sixth. Deploring his callousness, we are tempted to
admire his cheerful candour, and are almost touched by the emotional
poverty of his life.

At this impasse he takes the initiative, with the dissembling
announcement that he stands ready to be converted. His renunciation
is actually a temptation, to which the Friars easily succumb, enticed by
his Marlovian catalogue of the worldly goods he professes to renounce.

> Ware-houses stuft with spices and with drugs,
> Whole Chests of Gold, in *Bulloine*, and in Coyne...
> All this I'le giue to some religious house.   1573–84

Pretending to be persuaded, it is he who persuades and they who
do the courting. Their courtship is the most grotesque of Marlowe's
variations on the tune of 'Come live with me and be my love'. The
vistas of opulence that Barabas has just exhibited contrast with the
cheerless asceticism of their monkish vows. While Barabas ironically aspires toward grace, they fall into the trap of worldliness that he
has so lavishly baited for them.

> You shall conuert me, you shall haue all my wealth,   1590

he tells one. Whereupon the other tells him,

> Oh *Barabas*, their Lawes are strict...
> They weare no shirts, and they goe bare-foot too,   1591–3

and is told in turn,

> You shall confesse me, and haue all my goods.   1595

By playing off one monastic order against the other, he divides and
conquers. He murders one Friar and pins the blame on the other, with
a threadbare trick which Marlowe may have encountered in a jestbook.
The fact that the same trick occurs in a play of Thomas Heywood's,
The Captives, plus the fact that Heywood sponsored the publication
of *The Jew of Malta,* has led some commentators to infer that he may
have added these scenes to Marlowe's play. It would seem more prob-
able that *The Jew of Malta* influenced *The Captives.* Clearly it influenced *Titus Andronicus,* where the jest of a leaning corpse is men-
tioned by Aaron in his imitative monologue. . . .

It seems wiser—and is certainly more rewarding—to accept *The Jew
of Malta* as an artistic whole, noting its incongruities and tensions, than
to take the easy course of ruling them out as interpolations by a later
hand. Criticism is warranted in stressing the disproportion between the
two halves of the play; but the very essence of Marlowe's art, to sum
it up with a Baconian phrase, is 'strangenesse in the proportions'. The
'extreme reuenge' (1265) of Barabas runs away with the play,
egregiously transcending the norms of vindictiveness; but it is the

nature of the Marlovian protagonist to press whatever he undertakes to its uttermost extreme. As Barabas progresses, the Old Testament recedes into the background, and the foreground is dominated by *The Prince*. Effortlessly, his losses of the first act are made good by the second; and the third repays, with compound interest, his grudge against the Governor. Here, with the disaffection of Abigall, he abandons any claim upon our sympathy and vies with his new accomplice, Ithamore, in the *quid pro quo* of sheer malignity. In the fourth act he is blackmailed, not only by Bellamira and her bravo, but by the pair of Friars. His counter-measures lead him, in the fifth act, upward and onward into the realms of the higher blackmail, where Turks demand tribute from Christians and Christians from Jews.

> Why, was there euer seene such villany.
> So neatly plotted, and so well perform'd?   1220–1

Ithamore asks the audience. Yet who should know better than he, that the performance of each plot somehow leaves a loose end? Murder is not postponed from act to act, as it is in the bungling *Arden of Feversham*; rather, as in a well-conducted detective story, every crime is its own potential nemesis. Barabas does not count on Abigall's love for Mathias when he calculates the killing of Lodowick. He does away with her and her sister religionists without expecting the Friars to inherit his guilty secret. When he silences them, he comes to grips with the complicity of Ithamore and with the extortions of Pilia-Borza. In settling their business, he incriminates himself; and, though he survives to betray the entire island, his next and final treason is self-betrayal.

To show the betrayer betrayed, the engineer hoist in his petard, the 'reaching thought' (455) of Barabas overreached, is the irony of ironies. Marlowe's stage management moves toward a *coup de théâtre*, a machine which is worthy of all the machination that has gone before. Barabas can kill with a poisoned nosegay, can simulate death with 'Poppy and cold mandrake juyce' (2083), and—thrown to the vultures from the walls of the town—can let the enemy in through the underground vaults, the subterranean corridors of intrigue. His hellish broth for the nuns is brewed from the recipes of the Borgias, seasoned with 'all the poysons of the Stygian poole' (1405), and stirred with imprecations from the classics. 'Was euer pot of Rice porredge so sauc't?' comments Ithamore (1409). The sauce of the jest is that poetic justice takes, for Barabas, the shape of a boiling pot. He is shown *'aboue'*— from which coign of vantage he likes to look down on the havoc he engineers—*'very busie'* in his 'dainty Gallery' (2316), explaining his cable and trap-door to the Governor. When the signal is given, and the monastery blown up with the Turks inside, it is Barabas who falls through the trap. The curtain below is flung open, *'A Caldron discouered'*, and in it Barabas fuming and hissing his last. He implores the Christians to help him, but they are 'pittilesse' (2354). Once he mere y professed 'a burning zeale' (850), but now he feels 'the extremity of heat' (2371). He dies cursing. The steaming caldron in which he expires, like the 'hellmouth' of *Doctor Faustus,* was a property in the lists of Alleyn's company. But, like the human pie in *Titus Andronicus,* today it excites more ridicule than terror. In the age of *Macbeth,* however, a caldron was no mere object of domestic utility. It was the standard punishment for the poisoner. . . .

Barabas stews in the juice of his tragic pride, foiled and foiled again, like the melodramatic villain he has become. Malta is preserved; murder will out; crime does not pay; the reward of sin is death; vengeance belongs to the Lord. This is exemplary but commonplace doctrine, and we have clambered through a labyrinth to reach it. Can Machiavel's introductory proverbs of hell be conclusively refuted by such copybook didacticism? Barabas is a consistent Machiavellian when, at the very pinnacle of his career, he soliloquizes on Turks and Christians:

> Thus louing neither, will I liue with both,
> Making a profit of my policie.   2213–4

The words 'live' and 'love' jingle strangely amid this concentration of cold antipathy. Yet they are in character—or rather, Barabas steps out of it at the crisis, when he wilfully departs from the teaching of his master. Machiavelli, in his chapter on cruelty and pity, had counselled: 'Both dowbtlesse are necessarie, but seinge it is harde to make them drawe both in one yoake, I thinke it more safetie (seinge one must needes be wantinge) to be feared then loved, for this maybe boldlie sayde of men, that they are vngratefull, inconstante, discemblers, fearefull of dayngers, covetous of gayne.' This may unquestionably be said of Barabas, and he is all too painfully conscious of it; he is conscious of being hated, and wants to be loved. To be loved— yes, that desire is his secret shame, the tragic weakness of a character whose wickedness is otherwise unflawed. His hatred is the bravado of the outsider whom nobody loves, and his revenges are compensatory efforts to supply people with good reasons for hating him. Poor Barabas, poor old rich man! That he should end by trusting anybody, least of all the one man who wronged him in the beginning! He has authority now, but Malta hates him. Instead of playing upon the fear of the islanders, he proposes to earn their gratitude by ridding them of the Turks. As Governor, he is anxious to make his peace with the former Governor, to whom he says: 'Liue with me,' (2192). It is worse than a crime, as Talleyrand would say; it is a blunder.

The original miscalculation of Barabas was his failure to reckon with love. Then Abigall, sincerely professing the vows she had taken before out of policy, declared that she had found no love on earth. Having lost her, holding himself apart from the 'multitude' of Jews, Barabas must be his own sole friend: 'I'le looke vnto my selfe' (212).

Yet he would like to win friends; he needs a confidant; and for a while he views Ithamore, much too trustingly, as his 'second self' (1317). It is the dilemma of *unus contra mundum,* of the egoist who cannot live with others or without them. Since he conspires against them, they are right to combine against him, but their combinations frequently break down, for each of them is equally self-centred.

> For so I liue, perish may all the world.   2292

When every man looks out for himself alone and looks with suspicion on every other man, the ego is isolated within a vicious circle of mutual distrust. . . . The serpentine Barabas . . . comes to grief; and the difference between his caldron and Tamburlaine's chariot, between feeling pain and inflicting it, may well betoken Marlowe's advancing experience in the ways of the world. He is awakening to a vision of evil, though he innocently beholds it from the outside. The devil obligingly identifies himself by wearing horns and a tail.

But the devil is no diabolist; he sees through himself; he knows that men have invented him to relieve themselves of responsibility for those woes of the world which the Governor attributes to 'inherent sinne' (342). The devil's disciple, Machiavel, holds that there is no sin but ignorance; and Machiavel's disciple, Barabas, prefers the role of the knave to that of the fool. Thus, in letting other knaves get the better of him, he commits the only sin in his calendar, the humanistic peccadillo of folly. He acts out the Erasmian object lesson of a scoundrel who is too clever for his own good, the cheater cheated, wily beguiled. In getting out of hand, his counterplots exceeded the proportions of tragedy, and his discomfiture is more like the happy endings of melodrama. T. S. Eliot endows the play with a kind of retrospective unity by interpreting it as a comedy, a 'farce of the old English humour'. Though the interpretation is unhistorical, it has the merit of placing *The Jew of Malta* beside the grotesquerie of Dickens and Hogarth and—most pertinently—Ben Jonson's *Volpone, or the Fox.* Jonson's comedy of humours begins where Marlowe's tragedy of humours leaves off; Volpone and Mosca continue the misadventures of Barabas and Ithamore; and the Fox of Venice has learned not a few of his tricks from the Jew of Malta. . . .

The hard-bitten types of New Comedy are perennially recognizable: miser, impostor, parasite, prostitute. Whether in Malta or Venice, Athens or London, their outlook is always a street and never a landscape. Social intercourse is, for them, a commercial transaction; self-interest is the universal motive; everything, every man's honesty and every woman's, has its price; all try to sell themselves as dearly, and to buy others as cheaply, as possible. The moral issue is the simple choice between folly and knavery—in Elizabethan terms, the innocence of the gull and the wisdom of the coney-catcher. The distance between these extremes, as *The Jew of Malta* demonstrates, can be precariously narrow. Barabas, for all his monstrous activism, inhabits a small and static world. Though Marlowe would not be Marlowe without a cosmic prospect, he seems to be moving centripetally through a descending gyre toward a core of self-imposed limitation. But, even as potentialities seem to be closing in, actualities are opening up. The room is little, the riches are infinite.

From Chapter 3 of *The Overreacher: A Study of Christopher Marlowe*, Harvard University Press, Cambridge, 1952, pp. 56–80 (64–80).

F. P. WILSON

Edward II:
Ironies of Kingship

... In *Edward II* Marlowe is following the example which Shakespeare had already set: he goes to the English chronicles. Anyone who doubts whether Marlowe's gifts were really dramatic would do well to read Holinshed's account of the reign of Edward II and see with what art of selection, condensation, and adaptation Marlowe has shaped out of the chronicle history of a disagreeable reign an historical tragedy. The title suggests a chronicle: *The troublesome reign and lamentable death of Edward the Second, King of England: with the tragical fall of proud Mortimer*; but although history, especially in Acts II and III, is not wholly assimilated into drama, the running-title *The Tragedy of Edward the Second* represents the play better. Marlowe did not read so widely in the histories as did Michael Drayton for the 'Complaint' of Piers Gaveston written in the year of Marlowe's death, but he was not satisfied merely with Holinshed, and went elsewhere for many a detail: for example, the 'fleering' song with which the Scots mocked the English disgrace at Bannockburn, with its refrains 'With a heave and a ho', 'With a rombelow'. And he threw aside as unsuitable to his purposes much material connected with the wars of Scotland and Ireland and France, many a private war between baron and baron, and of course all those trivial disconnected details which the chronicles recorded. Moreover, historical dating and historical sequence he regarded as wholly within his control if it led to economy and coherence, above all if it led to the balance of dramatic power.

The balance of one character or motive with another is here essential, for this is his one play in which his purpose is to illustrate weakness, not strength. Weakness does not act but is acted upon, or if it acts its actions are frustrated and ineffective. Therefore Marlowe was forced by the nature of his theme to distribute the interest over a variety of characters as he never had occasion to do elsewhere, to exhibit not only the central figure of Edward in whom the play's intention is chiefly expressed but also the agents of power and corruption who act upon this figure. The stage is set for the conflict to follow in the four movements of the first scene. First, Gaveston just returned from banishment and eager to meet the King and to devise the sensuous pleasures which delight them both, a Gaveston who is not the mere self-seeker of the chronicles but as much infatuated with the King as the King with him, both men with a 'ruling desire' which counts the world well lost for love and pleasure. Secondly, the King's quarrel with the lords bitterly jealous of the upstart Gaveston, a quarrel overheard by Gaveston, a movement in which we meet the King's chief enemies, Lancaster, both Mortimers, and Warwick. Thirdly, the reunion of Edward and Gaveston. We are used in Shakespeare to the image of sea or river overflowing the land, as a symbol of chaos, an inversion of nature which is a token of evil in human nature; now the image is from Edward himself and marks the absence of all sense of kingly duty and moral scruple:

> I have my wish, in that I joy thy sight;
> And sooner shall the sea o'erwhelm my land,
> Than bear the ship that shall transport thee hence.
> > [Quotations are from *Edward II*,
> > ed. H. B. Charlton and R. D. Waller, 1933]

In a brief fourth movement Edward and Gaveston violently abuse the Bishop of Coventry and add to the hostility of the lords the powerful hostility of the Church. And so in the first scene, with great economy and power, Marlowe has introduced all the leading characters which are the necessary embodiments of his dramatic purpose except Queen Isabel: and she appears in the second scene. Of these characters Gaveston is murdered at the beginning of the third act; Lancaster is captured at the battle of Boroughbridge at the end of the third act; Mortimer and Isabel alone are as important in the last act as in the first; as the play proceeds their share in the personal tragedy of the King becomes increasingly important.

The part played by one character is too important to omit even in the briefest summary. Though of subsidiary importance the King's brother Edmund Earl of Kent fulfils a function in this play to which I think there is no parallel in Marlowe's other plays. Kent throws in his lot now with the King now with the King's enemies in a vain attempt to trim the ship of state. He is the one character in the play upon whom the affections can rest, the one character—apart from the young Prince Edward—whose concern for the King is wholly untouched by jealousy, hatred, lust or self-aggrandizement. This character is perhaps the only character in Marlowe's plays who may be regarded as a point of reference.

The similarity between the theme of *Edward II* and that of *Richard II*, written a few years later, is obvious: it must have been obvious to Shakespeare: he certainly knew Marlowe's play and he may have known it the better from having acted in it. In both characters there is fundamental weakness. It is not that there is a chink in their armour: they have no armour at all. In both characters there is change, but the change is not so much in them as in our feelings to them, as we see them passing from the cruelty and selfishness of power to the helplessness and suffering of powerlessness. But the similarities between these two plays are superficial. It is an altogether grimmer world into which Marlowe takes us, a world of evil and corruption deeper and darker than that of *Richard II*. The turning-point of Edward's fortunes comes with the death of Gaveston. Temporarily his fortunes recover with the victory at Boroughbridge, but the beginning of his end is the escape of Mortimer to France, whither the Queen and the young Edward have already been sent. Act IV shows Edward's defeat and capture by the forces led by Mortimer and Isabel.

The critics have attacked Marlowe for inconsistency in his portrayal of Mortimer and Isabel, but is there more inconsistency than dramatic poetry may claim? There is change, certainly, rather than development, but which dramatist of this date attempted to show development? And how very few attempted to show it later! We must not ask of an Elizabethan play what we ask of a naturalistic play. The change in Mortimer's character and in Isabel's is to add pity and terror to Edward's end, to assist in the swing from detestation and contempt of Edward when abusing his power to pity for Edward when he has fallen from high estate. Until the fourth act Mortimer is hardly distinguishable from the other proud and self-seeking lords: but as soon as Edward is defeated and the power falls into his own hands he becomes a Machiavel. 'Fear'd am I more than lov'd', and one of the maxims attributed to Machiavelli was that 'it is better for a Prince to be feared than loved'. Another maxim was that 'A man is happy so long as Fortune agreeth unto his nature and humour', and it is Mortimer and Mortimer alone who calls upon Fortune. At the height of his power he boasts that he makes Fortune's wheel turn as he pleases, and quotes from Ovid the line *Major sum quam cui possit fortuna nocere*. And when Edward's murder is brought home to him, and he sees that his end is in sight, there is no moral compunction but mere acquiescence in the decree of an arbitrary fate.

> Base Fortune, now I see, that in thy wheel
> There is a point, to which when men aspire,
> They tumble headlong down: that point I touch'd,
> And, seeing there was no place to mount up higher,
> Why should I grieve at my declining fall?
> Farewell, fair Queen: weep not for Mortimer,
> That scorns the world, and as a traveller
> Goes to discover countries yet unknown.

But it is the character of Edward's Queen Isabel that has proved the greatest stumbling-block to critics. Yet here again if we remember Marlowe's dramatic purpose and do not seek for realism, we shall find that he has not bungled a matter vital to the balance of his play, just as he made no mistake in departing from the chronicles which make no mention of an intrigue between Isabel and Mortimer before

Edward's murder. Of this intrigue we hear much in the first two acts, but always from Edward and Gaveston. They are not to be believed, and the effect of these slanders on the King's neglected Queen is to light up his unhallowed passion for his favourite, his privado.

> Like frantic Juno will I fill the earth
> With ghastly murmur of my sighs and cries;
> For never doted Jove on Ganymede
> So much as he on cursed Gaveston.

This the Queen speaks in soliloquy, and by the conventions of Elizabethan drama we are to suppose her speaking her inmost thoughts. Not until after repeated failures to win the affection of her husband, not until after her question 'No farewell to poor Isabel, thy Queen?' has received the brutal reply 'Yes, yes, for Mortimer, your lover's sake', does she betray the first hint of affection for Mortimer, again in soliloquy:

> So well hast thou deserv'd, sweet Mortimer,
> As Isabel could live with thee for ever.

But not yet has the moment arrived to swing the balance of pity towards Edward, and she continues:

> In vain I look for love at Edward's hand,
> Whose eyes are fix'd on none but Gaveston,
> Yet once more I'll importune him with prayers.

And if prayers fail, she will take refuge with her brother, the King of France. By this soliloquy we are prepared for her guilt, but she is not yet guilty. Marlowe keeps that in reserve until he needs it. And the first assurance of guilt is not given us until she and Mortimer have returned from France with their victorious army. Then this assurance *is* to be believed, for it is given us by Kent, whom I have called Marlowe's point of reference:

>   Mortimer
> And Isabel do kiss, while they conspire:
> And yet she bears a face of love forsooth.
> Fie on that love that hatcheth death and hate.

Now Isabel plays she-Machiavel to Mortimer's Machiavel. Cruel as well as unfaithful, she has nothing to learn in the art of turning and dissembling. In public she is full of concern for the state of the country and the King's misfortunes, of thanks to 'the God of kings' and 'heaven's great architect'; in private, there is no villainy of Mortimer's which she does not aid and abet.

It adds to the horror that in the last two acts Edward is never brought face to face with his two tormentors. The fear of their cruelty preys upon his mind in prison, fear as much for his son as for himself, and as in many an age besides Shakespeare's the cruelty of man and woman is expressed in terms of beasts of prey:

> For he's a lamb, encompassèd by wolves,
> Which in a moment will abridge his life.

And again,

> Let not that Mortimer protect my son;
> More safety is there in a tiger's jaws,
> Than his embracements.

The revulsion of feeling from contempt to pity is now complete, and it is in part the change in the characters of Mortimer and Isabel that has effected it.

> What, are you mov'd? pity you me?
> Then send for unrelenting Mortimer,
> And Isabel, whose eyes, being turn'd to steel,
> Will sooner sparkle fire than shed a tear.

At the end Edward is as terrified, as helpless, and as lonely as Faustus. But he is not penitent. Neither is Shakespeare's Richard II. . . . The chronicles present us with a penitent Edward, but this was not to Marlowe's purpose. Edward's thoughts are of Mortimer and of Isabel, of his own sorrows, his 'guiltless life', his 'innocent hands', and of the safety of his son:

> Commend me to my son, and bid him rule
> Better than I. Yet how have I transgress'd,
> Unless it be with too much clemency?

The humiliation and murder of Edward are narrated in full by the chroniclers. The details are sordid, pitiless, horrible. And Marlowe leaves out little. For one detail which he did not find in Holinshed, the washing and shaving of the King in puddle water, he went to Stow. Compassion did not come easily to Marlowe, and there is a cruelty in these last scenes which we do not find in Shakespeare. In *Richard II* there is every sort of alleviation. Richard is brought face to face with his accusers, and allowed to indulge himself in scenes which make him at once the playboy and the poet of the English kings. He takes affectionate farewell of his Queen—how different an Isabel from Edward's. In place of Mortimer we have a Bolingbroke. And at the end no passive submission, but death in courageous action. Shakespeare's compassion is nowhere more evident than in his invention of the faithful groom of the stable and the talk with his master about 'roan Barbary', when King and groom share a common humanity. In Marlowe there is no groom; instead, the invention of the murderer whom he christens, with a stroke of sardonic humour, Lightborn, the professional murderer who takes a pride in the fine handling of a

man. Into his taut-lipped lines Marlowe packs the quintessence of
all that Englishmen had heard or dreamt of Italianate villainy:

> You shall not need to give instructions;
> 'Tis not the first time I have killed a man.
> I learned in Naples how to poison flowers;
> To strangle with a lawn thrust through the throat;
> To pierce the windpipe with a needle's point;
> Or whilst one is asleep, to take a quill
> And blow a little powder in his ears;
> Or open his mouth and pour quicksilver down.
> But yet I have a braver way than these.

The 'braver way' is reported by the chronicles, but it was too strong
even for the stomach of an Elizabethan audience, and the red-hot spit
which Lightborn orders to be prepared is not called for. But the wail
of the murdered man rang through the theatre, as it did, writes
Holinshed,

> ... through the castle and town of Berkeley, so that divers being
> awakened therewith (as they themselves confessed) prayed heartily
> to God to receive his soul, when they understood by his cry what
> the matter meant.

Charles Lamb said that this death-scene moved pity and terror beyond any scene ancient and modern with which he was acquainted.
But I wonder if there is not too much horror in the terror, if the
scene is not so painful that it presses upon the nerves. In a short last
scene Mortimer and Isabel meet their doom, and the young King
Edward takes control. In the young Edward's words there is grief for
his father and righteous anger with the murderer, but the words rather
enforce the feeling that the dramatist does not deeply feel the sacredness of royalty, that the tragedy is in the main a personal tragedy
without wider repercussions, and that in the supporting characters he
has been exhibiting this and that variety of ambition, hatred, envy,
lust, and the corruption of men and women in power or in search of
power.

Marlowe's other heroes, except in *Dido* and *The Massacre at Paris,*
are men of humble birth: this is his one full study of kingship. He
is aware of the irony of kingship, and nowhere in this play is his
verse finer and fuller than in the abdication scene. When Shakespeare
came to write in *Richard II* of the 'reluctant pangs of abdicating
royalty' (the phrase is Lamb's), he remembered the scene, and well
he might, for in imagery and in pathos it is nearer to Shakespeare
than any other scene in Marlowe. But it stands almost alone in the
play as a scene in which Marlowe's poetic power is fully released.
When we have admitted that, we have admitted a weakness which no
care for craftsmanship can redeem. Marlowe never returned to the

theme of English history, as Shakespeare did again and again. He went on to write *Doctor Faustus* and there he fulfilled himself.

From *Marlowe and the Early Shakespeare*, Clarendon Press, Oxford, 1953, pp. 90–103.

G. WILSON KNIGHT

Marlowe's Limitations

... His people do not grow, as do Shakespeare's, through suffering. Tamburlaine becomes more and more repellent, the Jew disintegrates, Edward II is embarrassingly pathetic, and even Faustus's final declamation is no more than a sublime expression of terror. In Marlowe the most exquisite apprehensions are associated with the lascivious; he seems to be tormented by things at once hideously suspect yet tormentingly desirable, and he leaves us simultaneously aware of intoxication and degradation. His feminine interests are slight, and where there is humour it is cruel. He forecasts both Jonson and Milton and what he reveals is vastly important and deeply true. Yet revelation and truth are only half the tragic dramatist's task; the other half is transmutation, or catharsis, and this he does not master. His reach, admittedly titanic, exceeds his grasp....

From *The Golden Labyrinth: A Study of British Drama*, by G. Wilson Knight, W. W. Norton & Co., Inc., New York, 1962, pp. 54–9 (58–9).

CLIFFORD LEECH

Edward II:
Power and Suffering

...When he was writing *Edward II*, Marlowe was, I believe, much concerned with the ideas of power and suffering and the relation between the two, and it was this that led him to choose the subject. But during the actual process of composition what concerned him more directly was part of the spectacle of human life, the things that happened to Edward and Mortimer and Isabella and Gaveston. At times the impetus of their story led him indeed to ideas—like Fortune's wheel, the power of the Roman church, the 'unnaturalness' of rebellion, and the part played by Heaven in human affairs—that have little or no connection with the play's primary intellectual concern. Nevertheless, such ideas are there and clearly illustrate the multiplicity of statement that is typical of the drama of the time. In production, therefore, and in criticism, we should put our immediate stress on the thing that was most fully and persistently alive to the dramatist as he was writing, and that is the action and the human beings involved in it. Each character must be allowed to make his bid for our attention and our sympathetic response, despite the obvious fact that we shall be more interested in some than in others. The Marlowe Society [in their production of *Edward II* at Cambridge, Stratford-upon-Avon and London in 1958], giving us a performance in which we felt the diffused vitality of the human spectacle, seemed to make the play more available to us as a whole than it had previously been. On the stage, through the persons of the actors, we could become more deeply aware of the mental pressures exerted on Edward and Isabella and the rest. The play was their story, not a demonstration of the Tudor myth or of any private scheme thought out by Christopher Marlowe. Nearly all the best plays of the time have indeed this quality of objectivity, of belonging ultimately to their characters rather than to the dramatist. And contradictions, or at least dissonances, of ideas are as much at home in this drama as in our everyday conduct and thinking. When talking about the plays, we inevitably refer to the ideas that they suggest to us; but we must never forget that a dramatist, when writing, is normally concerned with such things only in the second place....

Marlowe...came in the writing of *Tamburlaine* to a fuller

perception of the things that went along with the possession of power
—its fragility, and the suffering that its free exercise involved. But in
Tamburlaine he was telling the story of a man wholly successful in
his conflicts with other men: the sufferings of the hero were merely
the operations of time or of Fortune's wheel or of cosmic justice. Now
we can assume that Parts II and III of *Henry VI* gave him a model
for a play differently centred. His main figure could still be a man of
power, but of power inherited not won, power insecurely held and ever
limited by the opposition of other men. This entailed his giving
greater prominence than in *Tamburlaine* to the subordinate figures in
the drama, and thus in *Edward II* he came closer to Shakespeare's
normal structural method than elsewhere in his writing. As in
Henry VI, the action was spread widely through the country, from
London to Tynemouth in the remote north and to Neath in South
Wales, and, as in Part III of *Henry VI*, there was a short excursion to
France. The effect of this in Marlowe is, however, different from what
we find in Shakespeare. In *Henry VI* it is justifiable to claim that the
diffusion of the action brings more fully into mind the sense of the
nation, and Henry's lament for his country's sufferings in Part III, II.v,
constitutes a key-passage for the play. But in Marlowe the idea of
the country and its war is very much in the background. *Edward II*
is a more personal play than *Henry VI*, and the rapid movement of the
action gives us the feeling of Edward being driven by the course of
events haphazardly through his realm, until at the end he is confined
to a small dark cell in which he is secretly murdered. It is as if all the
time that cell were waiting for him, and his long journeyings were
circuitous routes to that last place of suffering and humiliation.
Marlowe, we shall see, makes strong use of the passage in Holinshed
which says that he was continually taken, on Mortimer's orders, from
'one strong place to another, . . . still remoouing with him in the night
season':[1] these shorter journeys are the last stages of his wanderings,
until in the end even the motion stops and he is still at last. This
difference is related to the fact that Edward is a more important figure
in Marlowe's play than Henry is in Shakespeare's. For Shakespeare,
beyond Henry lie England and the doom she must suffer through civil
strife. For Marlowe, the concept of England means little—he was, after
all, a servant in Elizabeth's secret police—and he cared only for what
happened to the individual human being. He was interested in Edward,
not as embodying a suffering England, but as a man, a man who had
and lost power.

Yet it can be said that, at the beginning of the play, no one in
Edward II makes a good impression on us. First we meet Gaveston,
delighted to be recalled to England on Edward I's death. He makes
it plain that he has no love for the London to which he has returned:

[1] *The Historie of England* (vol. III), ed. 1585, p. 341.

> Not that I love the city, or the men,
> But that it harbours him I hold so dear,
> The king, upon whose bosom let me die,
> And with the world be still at enmity.   I. i. 12-15[2]

Then he encounters three 'Poor Men' who wish to enter his service: he behaves churlishly until he reminds himself that they may have their uses. Then in soliloquy he thinks of how he may 'draw the pliant king which way I please', and the devices he imagines show how he thinks to exploit Edward's homosexual leanings. When we meet the King and his nobles, we find Edward thinking only of Gaveston, whose worth we have already seen exposed, and the nobles pouring out their venom against him but with no indication that they have the country's good in mind. Then Edward and Gaveston meet, and we see Edward bestowing on him almost any office that comes into his mind:

> I here create thee Lord High Chamberlain,
> Chief Secretary to the state and me,
> Earl of Cornwall, King and Lord of Man.   I. i. 154-6

The King's brother, the Earl of Kent, though as yet wholly on Edward's side, protests:

> Brother, the least of these may well suffice
> For one of greater birth than Gaveston.   I. i. 158-9

Then we see Edward and Gaveston laying hands on the Bishop of Coventry, and the King sending him to prison and giving his see and revenues to Gaveston. Here we must recognize an ambivalence in Marlowe's attitude. The conduct of Edward and Gaveston is arbitrary and cruel, yet the references to the see of Rome and to the Bishop's wealth are in tune with the anti-Romish feeling which we find in *The Massacre at Paris* and which would awaken sympathetic echoes in many spectators of the time. As the first scene ended, the Elizabethan audience might well feel in two minds about the King and his favourite, being properly scandalized by their behaviour and yet taking in it a measure of delight.

In the second scene we meet Isabella, and her grief at Edward's desertion of her is likely to strengthen the audience's feeling against him. At once, however, we have a hint of a special relationship between the Queen and Mortimer. Her last words here are:

> Farewell, sweet Mortimer; and for my sake,
> Forbear to levy arms against the king.   I. ii. 81-2

We see her kindness for him ('sweet Mortimer') and her belief in having some power over him ('for my sake'), and also her wish for peace. But Mortimer's reply is brusque and has little love in it:

[2] Quotations from *Edward II* are from the edition of H. B. Charlton and R. D. Waller, 1933, revised ed. 1955.

> Ay, if words will serve; if not, I must.   I. ii. 83

When we see the King and the nobles together again, Edward is confronted with a demand for Gaveston's exile. This king has no concern for his country:

> Ere my sweet Gaveston shall part from me,
> This Isle shall fleet upon the Ocean,
> And wander to the unfrequented Inde.   I. iv. 48–50

He yields only because the Archbishop of Canterbury, as papal legate, threatens to release the nobles from their allegiance. And almost at once, as if this hint of Rome's power turns the scales, Marlowe gives Edward a line of verse that carries our sympathy to him. When Mortimer asks:

> Why should you love him whom the world hates so?   I. iv. 76

Edward's reply is simply:

> Because he loves me more than all the world.   I. iv. 77

We know what Gaveston's love is worth, yet this naïve utterance of Edward is enough to put us, for the moment, on his side: he becomes an emblem of the human need for love, the very human joy when love seems offered.

No sooner is Gaveston banished than the Queen persuades Mortimer, and through him the other lords, to consent to his recall. There is no hint yet of any infidelity on Isabella's part, yet she makes free use of her power over Mortimer, and Marlowe thus prepares us for a closer relationship between them. When the King learns that Gaveston may return, he entertains the kindest thoughts of the barons, and plans triumphs and revels. Then follows a significant conversation between Mortimer and his uncle. The older man counsels peace: 'The mightiest kings have had their minions,' he says, and quotes examples from history and mythology:

> Then let his grace, whose youth is flexible,
> And promiseth as much as we can wish,
> Freely enjoy that vain, light-hearted earl;
> For riper years will wean him from such toys.   I. iv. 397–400

Mortimer replies that he has no objection to Edward's wantonness:

> Uncle, his wanton humour grieves not me.   I. iv. 401

Rather, he will not tolerate Gaveston's enjoyment of riches idly bestowed on him and his mockery of those of more ancient lineage. It is true that Mortimer refers to 'the treasure of the realm' and to the fact that 'soldiers mutiny for want of pay', but in the speech as a whole there is little sense of the kingdom's good. The objection to

Gaveston is the common objection to an upstart, and this comes out clearly in Mortimer's final words in this scene:

> But whiles I have a sword, a hand, a heart,
> I will not yield to any such upstart.
> You know my mind; come, uncle, let's away.   I. iv. 421–3

There is no act division in the early copies of *Edward II*, but modern editors usually end Act I at this point. It is therefore convenient to sum up here our initial responses to the four main characters: Gaveston we know for a rogue, though a lively one; Mortimer is rough and self-centred, responsive, however, at moments to the Queen; Isabella is anxious for Edward's love, yet we can see she is playing dangerously with her power over Mortimer; Edward, we should know without history's warrant, is doomed: he can control neither his barons' unruliness nor his own blind passion.

We meet other associates of Gaveston at the beginning of the next scene. The younger Spencer and Baldock are servants in the household of the Earl of Gloucester, who has just died. The Earl's daughter, Edward's niece, is bethrothed to Gaveston: she is a rich heiress, another prize that the King will give to his favourite, and she has the misfortune to love Gaveston. Marlowe does not much develop this part of his story, possibly because to do so would over-dangerously emphasize the homosexual element. Yet we have seen enough of Edward's relations with Gaveston to find this marriage painful. But Marlowe does exhibit more fully the characters of Spencer and Baldock, and he lets us be under no illusion there. Spencer gives his fellow servant advice:

> You must be proud, bold, pleasant, resolute,
> And now and then stab, as occasion serves.   II. i. 42–3

And Baldock replies that he is

> inwardly licentious enough,
> And apt for any kind of villainy.   II. i. 50–1

To find equally frank avowals we must go to Marlowe's Jew of Malta or his Duke of Guise in *The Massacre at Paris* or to Shakespeare's Richard of Gloucester. These men are about to enter Gaveston's service and through him to serve the King, who welcomes them in the next scene. In that scene we have Gaveston's return and the immediate outbreak of fresh enmity: it ends with the barons' declaration of revolt and with Kent's abandoning his brother's cause. If we disregard act-division, for which, as we have seen, the early copies give us no warrant, we can regard this as the end of the play's first movement. From this point we have civil war, the barons fighting first for the removal of Gaveston and then for the removal of his successors in Edward's favour.

And at once there is a crucial moment in the presentation of Isabella. The King's forces are defeated, and Edward and Gaveston fly different ways in order to divide the barons' pursuing forces. Isabella is abandoned by her husband: she meets Mortimer and the rest, and tells them the route that Gaveston has taken. This is the first time she has acted against the King, and her final soliloquy in this scene shows how she hesitates between a new loyalty and an old hope to regain Edward's love:

> So well hast thou deserv'd, sweet Mortimer,
> As Isabel could live with thee for ever.
> In vain I look for love at Edward's hand,
> Whose eyes are fix'd on none but Gaveston,
> Yet once more I'll importune him with prayers:
> If he be strange and not regard my words,
> My son and I will over into France,
> And to the king my brother there complain,
> How Gaveston hath robb'd me of his love:
> But yet I hope my sorrows will have end,
> And Gaveston this blessed day be slain.   II. iv. 59–69

The change of Isabella from the wronged but loving wife to the woman acquiescent in her husband's murder has commonly been regarded as a blemish on the play. We should rather think of it, I suggest, as one of the most perceptive things in Marlowe's writing—at least in the planning, for one must admit that the words he gives her have not much life in them. Never before had he attempted the probing of a woman's character, for the presentation of Zenocrate, Olympia, Abigail, is for the most part emblematic. He knew a woman's frustrated love could turn rancid, as Dostoievsky shows in Katya's treachery to Mitya Karamazov, and Marlowe, like Dostoievsky, has not let the woman change without deep provocation. We have seen how she has long been conscious of Mortimer's feeling for her, how Mortimer for her is always 'gentle' or 'sweet' Mortimer, how Edward has taunted her with his love for Gaveston and accused her of infidelity. Now she finds herself deserted, with Edward's reproach still in her ears. This is the turning-point for her, though she does not know it yet. It is psychologically right that the moment of crisis should come without her realizing it.

In the scenes that follow we have Gaveston's capture, Edward's attempt to see him before he dies, and Warwick's brutal despatching of the favourite. There is an echo of Tamburlaine's blasphemy here. Marlowe's early hero had urged his soldiers to worship only 'the God that sits in heaven, if any god'. Now, when Gaveston asks 'Shall I not see the king?', Warwick replies: 'The king of heaven perhaps, no other king.' The scepticism of the 'perhaps' may be Marlowe's own, but the conduct of Warwick is base. Gaveston is allowed no eloquent last words, yet Marlowe suggests that he has a genuine desire to see Edward once more. There is at least no final stress on his villainy, and it is his killers who shock us and thus prepare us for their later barbarity to Edward. When the King hears of Gaveston's death, he vows revenge and in the same speech adopts Spencer as his new favourite, making him Earl of Gloucester and Lord Chamberlain— 'Despite of times, despite of enemies'. There is *hubris* in this, and yet almost at once Edward wins his first success in the play: he defeats the barons and takes them captive. Warwick and Lancaster are executed, going to their death with brief and obstinate words. Kent is sent away in disgrace, Mortimer committed to the Tower. Here Marlowe was in a difficulty; from Holinshed he knew that Mortimer had taken no part in this battle, having submitted to the King before it took place, but it would not do for him to follow his source in this regard, for Mortimer must throughout be the dominant figure among the barons. So we have the near-absurdity that Lancaster and Warwick are executed, while Mortimer, the most outspoken of the King's enemies and the suspected lover of the Queen, is given a further chance of life. This could have been avoided if Mortimer had been allowed to escape from the battlefield and to find his way at once to France. Probably, however, Marlowe wanted to suggest that Edward was a man incapable of profiting from Fortune's momentary favour. This temporary victory of the King brings the second movement of the play to an end. That Mortimer is alive and Isabella's loyalty now doubtful makes evident the continuing precariousness of Edward's position, and it is clear too that in replacing Gaveston by Spencer he has learned nothing.

Kent and Mortimer are soon in France, Mortimer having escaped from the Tower, and they meet Isabella and Prince Edward, who have been sent on an embassy to the French King. Together they plan new wars, nominally on behalf of the young prince. Quickly the scene returns to England, and Edward is defeated and a fugitive. With Spencer and Baldock he attempts flight to Ireland, but contrary winds drive him back to Wales. He takes refuge in the Abbey of Neath, but there he is quickly apprehended: Baldock and Spencer are taken to their deaths, the King to prison. Baldock, whom we first met as a villain in a puritan's disguise, is ready with rather hollow 'preachments', as his captor calls them, when he is led away to death. Marlowe has not much pity for these, though neither is he on their captors' side. In this scene, however, we have the beginning of the King's long journey to death. We have seen how he envies the monks their quiet life of contemplation, and when he hears the name of 'Mortimer' he shrinks and would hide his head:

> Mortimer, who talks of Mortimer?
> Who wounds me with the name of Mortimer,
> That bloody man? Good father, on thy lap

> Lay I this head, laden with mickle care.
> O might I never open these eyes again,
> Never again lift up this drooping head,
> O never more lift up this dying heart!   IV. vi. 37–43

When he takes his farewell of Spencer, he cannot believe that Heaven is punishing him:

> K. Edw.   Spencer, ah, sweet Spencer, thus then must we part.
> Spen. jun.   We must, my Lord, so will the angry heavens.
> K. Edw.   Nay, so will hell and cruel Mortimer;
>   The gentle heavens have not to do in this.   IV. vi. 72–5

Yet this denial of divine intervention is also in line with the general trend of the play's thought. There are few references to cosmic powers here: the conflict is on a purely human level, between a king who cannot control his lords or his passions and his unruly subjects who over-reach themselves. By the end of the play Isabella has been sent to the Tower and all the rest of the prominent characters are dead, but it is their folly, their mismanagement of the situation, that has destroyed them. The heavens, whether 'angry' or 'gentle', have it seems 'not to do in this'. But the scene of the King's capture is remarkable also for a piece of effective but unobtrusive symbolism. Before Mortimer's men arrive, Spencer has referred to a 'gloomy fellow in a mead below', who 'gave a long look after us', and it is this 'gloomy fellow' who betrays them. The stage-directions call him 'a Mower', and we must assume he comes carrying his scythe. At the end of the scene, when the King has been taken to prison and Baldock and Spencer are about to be put to death, the Mower asks for his reward. He has had only two lines to speak, but his presence on the stage makes it evident that the King is being cut down.

The abdication scene follows. There is no stress here on any sacredness in the idea of royalty, no suggestion of woe falling upon the land because of an act of deposition. But there is great poignancy in Edward's relinquishing of his crown. Like Faustus, shortly before or shortly after this play was written, he wishes time to stand still. 'Stay awhile, let me be king till night', he says, and then would have the day not cease:

> Stand still you watches of the element;
> All times and seasons, rest you at a stay,
> That Edward may be still fair England's king.   V. i. 66–8

An ironic touch of legality is given to the affair in that it is the Bishop of Winchester who comes to demand the crown, and when Edward proves obstinate, he is told that his son will 'lose his right'. He prays to be able to 'despise this transitory pomp And sit for aye enthronized in heaven'. For a moment he admits his guilt, but at once retracts the admission:

Commend me to my son, and bid him rule
Better than I. Yet how have I transgress'd,
Unless it be with too much clemency?   V. i. 121–3

Marlowe could enter fully into the mind of a man whose power was
slipping away from him. He had shown Tamburlaine in his attempt to
build his power on surer foundations than life allows and in his final
vain persuasion of himself that his sons would reign and conquer in his
behalf. Now he shows us a king bereft of his crown, the symbol of
the power already lost. Yet even that symbol was some kind of protec-
tion. As soon as it is gone, Edward is told of a change in his jailor and
his place of imprisonment. Further changes are to come, and each
for the worse. From the Earl of Leicester he is given to Sir Thomas
Berkeley, and then to Gurney and Matrevis, and finally to Marlowe's
fictitious executioner, Lightborn.

The remaining scenes alternate between the court, where
Mortimer, now Lord Protector and the Queen's lover, is all-powerful
but intent, for safety's sake, on the King's death, and the places where
Edward and his jailors are. The barbarity of these latter scenes makes
them painful to read or to see or to speak of. No other tragic figure
in Elizabethan or Jacobean times is treated in the degrading way that
Mortimer permits for Edward. Henry VI is suddenly stabbed,
Richard II dies fighting and eloquent, Richard III and Macbeth are
killed in battle, the Duchess of Malfi makes a brave and pious speech
before she is strangled, Marlowe's own Faustus dominates the scene
in his hour of despair.[3] The Jacobean playwrights could think of
strange ways of torment and murder, but they never tear at our
nerves as Marlowe does in this play. First we have the brief scene in
which the King, on his journeying with Matrevis and Gurney, begs
for water to drink and to clean his body. Their response is to take water
from a ditch, pour it over the King's face and shave off his beard. In
the last scene in which he appeared, Edward had been robbed of his
crown: now he is further stripped, is nearer the ultimate humiliation.
This incident of the shaving is not in Holinshed. Marlowe found it in
Stow's *Annals*,[4] and it is significant that he decided here to supplement
his primary source. The scene of the murder is dominated by the
figure of Lightborn, who comes with Mortimer's commission. This is
the professional murderer, devoid of pity but curiously intimate with
his victim. He pretends to sorrow for the King's wretched state, and
urges him to rest. Edward is half-ready to trust him, yet can sleep only
for a moment, his fears returning strongly upon him:

    [3] Especially in the A-text (1604), which W. W. Greg has seen as a corrupt
version of Marlowe's final handling: cf. *Marlowe's Doctor Faustus* 1604–16:
Parallel Texts, Oxford 1950, esp. pp. 129–32.
    [4] Cf. *The Annales of England*, ed. 1592, p. 343, where the incident is recorded
with the marginal gloss 'King Edward shauen with colde water'. Cf. *Edward II*,
ed. H. B. Charlton and R. D. Waller, revised ed. 1955, pp. 50, 191–2.

> Something still buzzeth in mine ears,
> And tells me if I sleep I never wake;
> This fear is that which makes me tremble thus;
> And therefore tell me, wherefore art thou come?   V. v. 102-5

Then he has only two brief speeches more:

> I am too weak and feeble to resist:
> Assist me, sweet God, and receive my soul!   V. v. 107-8

and:

> O spare me, or despatch me in a trice.   V. v. 110

And then the murder is done. The manner of its doing has been softened by most editors, who have inserted a form of stage-direction not in the early copies. There can, I think, be no doubt that Marlowe intended the mode of killing to be that narrated in Holinshed and clearly indicated by Lightborn in his talk with the jailors at the beginning of the scene. That indeed is how it was staged in the recent Marlowe Society production, and I think rightly. The mode of killing may have been one of the reasons why Marlowe chose this story for dramatization. We have seen how in *Tamburlaine* he could hint at something near the ultimate in human suffering in referring to the fate of the kings who drew their conqueror's chariot. In *Faustus* he imagined damnation. Here in *Edward II* he stages the ultimate physical cruelty. He was a man who speculated on, and brought alive to his mind, the furthest reaches of human power and of human suffering and humiliation. These things, he saw, men could do and had done, could suffer and had suffered, and his wondering mind gave them dramatic shape. And 'the gentle heavens have not to do in this'. There is no justice which works in this way.

Not so long ago it was possible for readers of Marlowe, and of the dramatists who followed him, to look on such scenes as relics of a barbarous though brilliant age. We have not today that way out, for evidence is plentiful that in this twentieth century there are Lightborns enough. I do not think that, when he wrote the play, Marlowe had a moral purpose: he was intent only on the imagining of an ultimate in suffering. Such imaginings are dangerous, for a cruelty grown familiar is the greatest corrupter. Nevertheless, Marlowe has brought before us part of the truth about men, and we must learn to recognize and to control it.

In the last scene of the play Fortune's wheel turns for Mortimer and Isabella, and the young King mourns for his father. This is briefly and almost casually done. It was necessary that the story of Edward's reign should be rounded off, and that Mortimer's stratagems should entrap him. But Marlowe's interest in this was not profound. He had traced with some care the working of power's corruption in Mortimer and the slow hardening of Isabella's heart, but he could part with them as perfunctorily as with Gaveston or Spencer. There is indeed a rather empty rhetoric in Mortimer's acceptance of the turning wheel and his readiness for what may come:

> Farewell, fair queen; weep not for Mortimer,
> That scorns the world, and, as a traveller,
> Goes to discover countries yet unknown.   V. vi. 64–6

Certainly it would be difficult to find two other lovers in Elizabethan drama who parted with words so chill.

In this play the final impression is of Edward's suffering. It is bound up with power, the power that Edward loses, the power that Mortimer wins, the power he delegates to Lightborn. If a man had no power over other men, there could be no suffering such as Edward knew. There could be other forms of anguish, but not this. And Marlowe, in a story where there was much to interest him, comes into full command of his imagination when he considers the last stages of Edward's journey. The association of the King and Gaveston, the process of Isabella's inconstancy, the barons' resentment of the favourite of humble origin, the slow transformation of Mortimer from a quarrelsome noble to a ruthless autocrat, the changing loyalties of Kent, the lightly sketched relations of the royal and the papal power— all these are part of the play, and they help to give to it the solidity of the world we know. Nevertheless, these things form the setting for the individual Edward's solitary journey to his end. And for Edward Marlowe does not ask our liking: he is foolish, he is at his best pathetic in the belief that Gaveston loves him more than all the world, he is cruel to his wife and drives her to Mortimer, he knows himself so little that he thinks he erred only in too much clemency. There is barely a redeeming moment in the long presentation of his conduct. Yet what Marlowe has done is to make us deeply conscious of a humanity that we share with this man who happened to be also a king. If there were a touch of greatness or even much kindness in him, as there is in Shakespeare's Richard II, we could remember that along with his suffering and find some comfort in it. As it is, we know only that he has human folly and in his suffering makes contact with an ultimate.

There is no theory here which Marlowe illustrates, no warning or programme for reform, no affirmation even of a faith in man. The playwright merely focuses attention on certain aspects of the human scene. In *Tamburlaine* he had already contemplated power, and saw that the spectacle inevitably included suffering. Here the suffering, still consequential on the exercise and the dream of power, is the major fact.

From 'Marlowe's *Edward II*: Power and Suffering', The Ann Elizabeth Sheble Lecture, Bryn Mawr College, 1958, in *The Critical Quarterly*, vol. I, no. 3, 1959, pp. 181-96 (182-3, 186-96).

LEO KIRSCHBAUM

Dr Faustus:
A Reconsideration

... *Outside* the theatre, we may mightily agree or disagree with the
eschatology inherent in *Doctor Faustus*. But *in* the theatre, as we
watch the play, we understand and accept (if only for the nonce)
that man's most precious possession is his immortal soul and that he
gains Heaven or Hell by his professions and actions on earth. *In*
the theatre, we accept Marlowe's premises. That these premises were
inherent in his first audience is of incidental interest to us as students
and appreciators of the drama. The premises are instinct in every
word, line, passage, speech, action of the play. The Christian view
of the world informs *Doctor Faustus* throughout—not the pagan view.
If we do not accept that Faustus's selling his soul to the devil for
earthly power and pleasure is a serious business, we simply are not
hearing what Marlowe wrote.

Critics confound Marlowe the man and Marlowe the playwright.
They consider that the man was an atheist and so interpret *Doctor
Faustus*. What if the play were anonymous? What has biography to
do with a play we are presumably watching in the theatre? Whatever
Marlowe was himself, there is no more obvious Christian document
in all Elizabethan drama than *Doctor Faustus*. Or critics will consider
the protagonist as a representative of the Renaissance superman. Whatever their feelings and thoughts on the revival of learning and the
Reformation are, let them open-mindedly look at the play unfolding
on the stage before them. For earthly learning, earthly power, earthly
satisfaction, Faustus goes down to horrible and everlasting perdition.
It does not matter what *you* think of Hell or what Marlowe privately
thought of Hell. What does matter is that in terms of the play,
Faustus is a wretched creature who for lower values gives up higher
values—that the devil and Hell are omnipresent, potent, and terrifying realities. These are the values which govern the play. You must
temporarily accept them while you watch the play. You need not
ultimately accept them. But you should not interpret the play in the
light of *your* philosophy or religion or absence of religion. You
cannot do so if you hear it properly—as a play, as an entity, as a
progressive action, as a quasi-morality in which is clearly set forth the
hierarchy of moral values which enforces and encloses the play, which

the characters in the play accept, which the playwright advances and accepts in his prologue and epilogue, which—hence—the audience must understand and accept.

Now I want to apply what has been said above to the following famous speech from Doctor Faustus (V. i. 107–26):

> Was this the face that launch'd a thousand ships,
> And burnt the topless towers of Ilium?—
> Sweet Helen, make me immortal with a kiss.—
> Her lips suck forth my soul; see where it flies!—
> Come, Helen, come, give me my soul again.
> Here will I dwell, for heaven is in these lips,
> And all is dross that is not Helena.   *Enter old man*
> I will be Paris, and for love of thee,
> Instead of Troy, shall Wittenberg be sack'd;
> And I will combat with weak Menelaus,
> And wear thy colours on my plumed crest:
> Yea, I will wound Achilles in the heel,
> And then return to Helen for a kiss.
> O, thou art fairer than the evening's air
> Clad in the beauty of a thousand stars;
> Brighter art thou than flaming Jupiter
> When he appear'd to hapless Semele;
> More lovely than the monarch of the sky
> In wanton Arethusa's azured arms;
> And none but thou shalt be my paramour!   *Exeunt.*[1]

This passage has again and again been presented in appreciation of Marlowe. 'What a marvellous pæan to beauty!' say the critics. Is it? Let us examine it in its context.

The reader will forgive a rapid survey of the play—which is necessary because of prevalent misunderstanding of Marlowe's artistic purpose in the drama. Necessarily, over-simplification must result, but major inaccuracy will not, I hope, be present.

The playwright immediately tells us in the Prologue:

> So much he profits in divinity,
> That shortly he was grac'd with Doctor's name,
> Excelling all and sweetly can dispute
> In th' heavenly matters of theology;
> Till swoln with cunning, of a self-conceit,
> His waxen wings did mount above his reach,
> And, melting, heavens conspir'd his over-throw;

---

[1] I employ the 1616 (B) text but have availed myself of the act, scene, line numbering; normalized spelling; lineation; stage-directions; and speech prefixes of F. S. Boas's edition. Since his is an eclectic text, I have had to make a few changes here and there—none material. I follow the 1604 (A) text in five places: II. ii. 20–2 and 100–2 which are not in B; the second half-line of V. i. 78; the entrance of the Old Man in the midst of the Helen eulogy, V. i. 113; and the Old Man's speech V. i. 127–9. The Old Man does not reappear in B after his exhortation.

> For, falling to a devilish exercise,
> And glutted now with learning's golden gifts,
> He surfeits upon cursed necromancy;
> Nothing so sweet as magic is to him,
> Which he prefers before his chiefest bliss:
> And this the man that in his study sits.

We *must* trust Marlowe's *ex cathedra* description of his protagonist—
a man who, swollen with pride in his attainments, comes to a deserved
end because he has preferred forbidden pursuits to 'his chiefest bliss'.
(Certainly Marlowe guides us deftly by the analogy with Icarus—who,
of course, equates with Lucifer; see below I. iii. 67–71.) The Faustus
whom Marlowe gives us in the ensuing action is both more complex
and less radiant than the utterances of scholars would lead us to
expect.

That thus and so the world is constituted, that given a certain
act of moral and spiritual significance such a consequence will follow,
is indicated implicitly not only by the occurrences of the play but
also explicitly by the choruses (as we have seen); by Faustus's own
recognition; by Mephistophilis; by the Scholars; by the Old Man
(perhaps the most important guide Marlowe supplies us), etc. A chief
device of such exposition is the Good Angel, the voice of God, the
expounder of things as they are—who always appears in concert with
the Bad Angel, the emissary of the Devil. Thus, at the very beginning
of Faustus's temptation, the Good Angel says (I. i. 71–4):

> O, Faustus, lay that damned book aside,
> And gaze not on it, lest it tempt thy soul,
> And heap God's heavy wrath upon thy head!
> Read, read the Scriptures:—that is blasphemy.

But Faustus hearkens to the Bad Angel. And note what he expects as
a reward for practising the forbidden black magic. Before the Good
Angel enters, he gloats (I. i. 54–6):

> O, what a world of profit and delight,
> Of power, of honour, and omnipotence,
> Is promised to the studious artizan!

After this entrance, he further reveals his expectations. He will not
only get knowledge and power: his mind dwells longingly on satisfaction of material appetite. The spirits will bring him 'gold', 'orient
pearl', 'pleasant fruits', 'princely delicates', 'silk' (I. i. 83–92).

Not only has Faustus intellectual pride to an odious degree, but he
is also avid for more vainglory (I. i. 113–9):

> And I, that have with subtle syllogisms
> Gravell'd the pastors of the German church,
> And made the flowering pride of Wittenberg
> Swarm to my problems, as the infernal spirits

> On sweet Musæus when he came to hell,
> Will be as cunning as Agrippa was,
> Whose shadows made all Europe honour him.

Faustus is wholly egocentric. To himself, he is either the greatest of men or the greatest of abject sinners. He underrates his opponents, and relishes his inflated sense of his own abilities. Thus, after Mephistophilis has left the stage at the behest of the magician that he reappear in the more pleasant guise of a Franciscan (Marlowe is indeed subtle: Faustus will not and can not accept things as they are: the truth must be side-stepped some way, the bitter pill must be coated with sugar), Faustus wallows in a delusion of self-importance (I. iii. 31–3):

> How pliant is this Mephistophilis,
> Full of obedience and humility!
> Such is the force of magic and my spells....

But Mephistophilis quickly disillusions him (I. iii. 47–56):

> *Faust.* Did not my conjuring raise thee? speak?
> *Meph.* That was the cause, but yet *per accidens*;
> For, when we hear one rack the name of God,
> Abjure the Scriptures and his Saviour Christ,
> We fly, in hope to get his glorious soul;
> Nor will we come, unless he use such means
> Whereby he is in danger to be damn'd.
> Therefore the shortest cut for conjuring
> Is stoutly to abjure all godliness,
> And pray devoutly to the prince of hell.

Faustus agrees to worship Belzebub (I. iii. 61–5):

> This word 'damnation' terrifies not me,
> For I confound hell in Elysium:
> My ghost be with the old philosophers!
> But, leaving these vain trifles of men's souls
> Tell me what is that Lucifer thy lord!

But note how Marlowe immediately shows up the vanity and fool-hardiness of this last speech. In order to set forth that damnation and soul are not mere trifles, the playwright has the enemy of man strip Faustus of those very delusions which the enemy of man wants Faustus to possess in order that the enemy of man may destroy Faustus. This dramatic device is similar to that of disjunct character which I discussed earlier: the enemy of the truth supports the truth so that the audience will be absolutely clear as to what the truth is. And note that Mephistophilis foreshadows Faustus's fall in Lucifer's, and that insolence and pride are the instigators in both cases (I. iii. 67–84):

Faust. Was not that Lucifer an angel once?
Meph. Yes, Faustus, and most dearly lov'd of God.
Faust. How comes it then that he is prince of devils?
Meph. O, by aspiring pride and insolence;
          For which God threw him from the face of heaven.
Faust. And what are you that live with Lucifer?
Meph. Unhappy spirits that fell with Lucifer,
          Conspir'd against our God with Lucifer,
          And are for ever damn'd with Lucifer.
Faust. Where are you damn'd?
Meph.   In hell.
Faust. How comes it then that thou art out of hell?
Meph. Why this is hell, nor am I out of it:
          Think'st thou that I, that saw the face of God,
          And tasted the eternal joys of heaven,
          Am not tormented with ten thousand hells,
          In being depriv'd of everlasting bliss?
          O, Faustus, leave these frivolous demands,
          Which strikes a terror to my fainting soul!

But the foolhardy Faustus, having been warned by the Devil himself, reprimands the latter for cowardliness! He boasts (I. iii. 85–8):

          What, is great Mephistophilis so passionate
          For being deprived of the joys of heaven?
          Learn thou of Faustus manly fortitude,
          And scorn those joys thou never shalt possess.

How can any one read the scene and call the self-deluded, foolishly boastful Faustus a superman?

Note carefully what Faustus wants in return for selling his soul to the devil (I. iii. 92–9):

          Say, he surrenders up to him his soul,
          So he will spare him four-and-twenty years,
          Letting him live in all voluptuousness;
          Having thee ever to attend on me,
          To give me whatsoever I shall ask,
          To tell me whatsoever I demand,
          To slay mine enemies, and to aïd my friends,
          And always be obedient to my will.

Utter satisfaction of the will and utter satisfaction of the senses are what Faustus desires. And how he prates (I. iii. 104–5)—who a little later will be quaking!

          Had I as many souls as there be stars,
          I'd give them all for Mephistophilis.

The next time we see Faustus, midnight of the same day, his emotional and intellectual instability is fully revealed. He veers between God and the Devil. At first, he is conscience-stricken. All

his cocky effrontery is gone. But in a moment he is once more the user
of egocentric hyperbole (II. i. 1–14):

> Now, Faustus, must
> Thou needs be damn'd. Canst thou not be sav'd?
> What boots it, then, to think on God or heaven?
> Away with such vain fancies, and despair;
> Despair in God, and trust in Belzebub:
> Now go not backward; Faustus, be resolute:
> Why waver'st thou? O, something soundeth in mine ear,
> 'Abjure this magic, turn to God again!'
> Ay, and Faustus will turn to God again.
> Why, he loves thee not;
> The God thou serv'st is thine own appetite,
> Wherein is fix'd the love of Belzebub:
> To him I'll build an altar and a church,
> And offer lukewarm blood of new-born babes.

A weakling, he must cover his fears with megalomaniacal fantasy.
Two points should be made. We must understand that Faustus's conclusion as to the impossibility of God's mercy is the mark of a diseased
ego—a lack of humility. And also, we must particularly remark
Faustus's self-recognition of his driving passion: 'The God thou
serv'st is thine own appetite'.

The struggle between Faustus's uncontrolled appetite and the
powers of Heaven continues (II. i. 15–26):

> *Enter the two Angels.*
>
> *Bad Ang.* Go forward, Faustus, in that famous art,
> *Good Ang.* Sweet Faustus, leave that execrable art.
> *Faust.* Contrition, prayer, repentance—what of these?
> *Good Ang.* O, they are means to bring thee unto heaven!
> *Bad Ang.* Rather illusions, fruits of lunacy,
> That makes them foolish that do use them most.
> *Good Ang.* Sweet Faustus, think of heaven and heavenly things.
> *Bad Ang.* No, Faustus; think of honour and of wealth.
>   [*Exeunt Angels.*
> *Faust.* Wealth! Why, the signiory of Embden shall be mine.
> When Mephistophilis shall stand by me,
> What power can hurt me? Faustus, thou art safe:
> Cast no more doubts—

He thus deludes himself. But again Faustus is warned by the emissary
of Hell what awaits him if he sells his soul to the Devil (II. i. 38–44):

> *Faust.* Stay, Mephistophilis, and tell me what good
> Will my soul do thy lord?
> *Meph.* Enlarge his kingdom.
> *Faust.* Is that the reason why he tempts us thus?
> *Meph.* *Solamen miseris socios habuisse doloris.*
> *Faust.* Why, have you any pain that torture others?
> *Meph.* As great as have the human souls of men.

And that Faustus has free will, free choice, ability to affirm or deny God if he so wishes; that he cannot (as he does later) blame anyone but himself for his act and its consequences, Faustus himself makes clear when, after his blood has congealed so that he cannot sign the document and give his soul to Hell, he says (II. i. 66–9):

> Why streams it not, that I may write afresh?
> *Faustus gives to thee his soul:* oh, there it stay'd!
> Why shouldst thou not? is not thy soul thine own?
> Then write again, *Faustus gives to thee his soul.*

Marlowe's powers of compressed dramatic irony can be tremendous. As soon as Faustus has signed, he says '*Consummatum est*' (II. i. 74), the last words of Christ on earth according to St John. What an insight into the twisted mind of the magician! And what blasphemy! Jesus died that Faustus's soul might live; Faustus flings away this priceless gift for a mess of earthly pottage! But the words are also true in a more literal sense: the good life, the possibility of reaching Heaven, are indeed finished for Faustus.

When, immediately afterward, God's warning '*Homo, fuge!*' appears on Faustus's arm, he—characteristically—affirms the God whom he has just denied and gets into a turmoil of conflicting impulses (II. i. 77–81):

> *Homo fuge!* Whither should I fly?
> If unto God, he'll throw me down to hell.
> My senses are deceiv'd: here's nothing writ:—
> O yes, I see it plain; even here is writ,
> *Homo fuge!* Yet shall not Faustus fly.

Hence, Faustus consciously and deliberately sets his will against God's. But as he is in this state, Mephistophilis, knowing his victim, says in an aside, 'I'll fetch him somewhat to delight his mind' (II. i. 82). And then to the voluptuary (II. i. 82–90),

> *Enter Devils, giving crowns and rich apparel to Faustus.*
> *They dance, and then depart.*

> *Enter* MEPHISTOPHILIS.

Faust.	What means this show? Speak, Mephistophilis.
Meph.	Nothing, Faustus, but to delight thy mind,
	And let thee see what magic can perform.
Faust.	But may I raise such spirits when I please?
Meph.	Ay, Faustus, and do greater things than these.
Faust.	Then, Mephistophilis, receive this scroll,
	A deed of gift of body and of soul ...

Thus, Mephistophilis deliberately offers Faustus sensual satisfaction in order to distract his mind from spiritual concern which might, of course, lead to repentance. This pattern is a basic one in the play, and an understanding of it will eventually enable us to interpret truly the Helen of Troy apostrophe. Whenever there is danger (from the Devil's viewpoint) that Faustus will turn to God's mercy, the powers of Hell will deaden their victim's conscience by providing him with some great satisfaction of the senses. But sometimes Faustus will ask for the opiate himself.

In the same scene, Faustus receives a true description of his condition, but cheaply flaunts his disbelief—as though one should deny gravity! Once more it is Mephistophilis who forcefully establishes the eschatology and values (II. i. 128–38):

Faust. I think hell's a fable.
Meph. Ay, think so, till experience change thy mind.
Faust. Why, dost thou think that Faustus shall be damn'd?
Meph. Ay, of necessity, for here's the scroll
　　　In which thou hast given thy soul to Lucifer.
Faust. Ay, and body too: but what of that?
　　　Think'st thou that Faustus is so fond to imagine
　　　That, after this life, there is any pain?
　　　No, these are trifles and mere old wives' tales.
Meph. But I am instance to prove the contrary;
　　　For I tell thee I am damn'd, and now in hell.

And here, again, Marlowe shows the constitution of Faustus's mind. As soon as Mephistophilis has stated that hell with its tortures and damnation do exist, Faustus asks for his customary anodyne for uncomfortable conscience (II. i. 139–56):

Faust. Nay, and this be hell, I'll willingly be damn'd:
　　　What! sleeping, eating, walking, and disputing!
　　　But, leaving this, let me have a wife,
　　　The fairest maid in Germany, for I
　　　Am wanton and lascivious
　　　And cannot live without a wife.
Meph. Well, Faustus, thou shalt have a wife.
　　　　　He fetches in a woman-devil.
Faust. What sight is this?
Meph. Now, Faustus, wilt thou have a wife?
Faust. Here's a hot whore indeed! No, I'll no wife.
Meph. Marriage is but a ceremonial toy:
　　　And if thou lovest me, think no more of it.
　　　I'll call thee out the fairest courtesans,
　　　And bring them ev'ry morning to thy bed:
　　　She whom thine eye shall like, thy heart shall have,
　　　Were she as chaste as was Penelope,
　　　As wise as Saba, or as beautiful
　　　As was bright Lucifer before his fall.

See again Marlowe's compressed irony—Faustus shall have his appetite satisfied by women as beautiful 'as was bright Lucifer before his fall'.

In the next scene (II. ii.), the Devil's agent and Faustus are again together. Faustus is going through another of his struggles between repentance and non-repentance. He blames Mephistophilis for his misery (2–3), but the latter points out that the magician made his choice of his own free-will: "Twas thine own seeking, Faustus, thank thyself' (4). When Faustus says that he 'will renounce this magic and repent' (11), he himself in a lucid moment recognizes that repentance is still possible. And the Good Angel at once announces also that a true act of contrition followed by God's forgiveness can still occur (12). But continued exercise in sin is robbing Faustus of volition —'My heart is hardened, I cannot repent' (18). However, this too must be taken as an egocentric conclusion. No sooner does he think of holy things, than the assertion 'Faustus, thou art damn'd' thunders in his ears (19–21). And all kinds of instruments for self-destruction are placed before him (21–3). Then in self-revelation he gives us another sharp insight into his essential make-up (24–5):

> And long ere this I should have done the deed,
> Had not sweet pleasure conquer'd deep despair.

As I have pointed out, sensuous pleasure is always Faustus's remedy for spiritual despair. He has had Homer and Orpheus sing for him (25–9). And now the very thought of former pleasure drugs his conscience (31–2):

> Why should I die, then, or basely despair?
> I am resolv'd; Faustus shall not repent.

It is instructive to compare Macbeth with Faustus. The former is tremendous in his spiritual agony. But the Faustus who, here and elsewhere, goes through such rapid mental and emotional gyrations is surely conceived of by his creator as of infinitely smaller dimension.

In the latter part of this scene (II. ii.) there is almost a replica of the pattern of the first part of the scene. Mephistophilis tells Faustus: 'thou art damn'd; think thou of hell' (75). And the latter once more characteristically blames Lucifer's servant for his plight: "Tis thou hast damn'd distressed Faustus' soul' (79). And so once more the protagonist is in spiritual distress. The Good Angel tells him there is still time to repent (82). But the Bad Angel promises, 'If thou repent, devils will tear thee in pieces' (83). (We must remember that the obverse of love of pleasure is fear of pain.) Just as Faustus calls upon his Saviour for help (85–6), Lucifer, Belzebub, and Mephistophilis enter. Lucifer appears menacing and frightening (89):

Faust. O, what art thou that look'st so terribly?

And after a few lines of prodding (87–97), the wretchedly irresolute hedonist once more veers and blatantly boasts (99–102):

> never to look to heaven,
> Never to name God, or to pray to him,
> To burn his Scriptures, slay his ministers,
> And make my spirits pull his churches down.

Once again the Devil gets Faustus out of his melancholy by providing him with some satisfaction of the senses—the show of the Seven Deadly Sins. Note again Marlowe's dramatic irony (109–11):

> That sight will be as pleasant to me,
> As Paradise was to Adam, the first day
> Of his creation.

And after the show, the deluded magician in unconscious irony says (173), 'O, how this sight doth delight my soul.'

In III. i. at the beginning of the anti-papist scene, we have another statement by Faustus of his motivating passion (58–62):

> Sweet Mephistophilis, thou pleasest me,
> Whilst I am here on earth, let me be cloy'd
> With all things that delight the heart of man.
> My four-and-twenty years of liberty
> I'll spend in pleasure and in dalliance,

And in IV. v. the Horse-Courser scene, Marlowe shows the protagonist still tormented—but still capable of rapid self-delusion (23–8):

> What art thou, Faustus, but a man condemn'd to die?
> Thy fatal time draws to a final end,
> Despair doth drive distrust into my thoughts.
> Confound these passions with a quiet sleep.
> Tush! Christ did call the thief upon the Cross;
> Then rest thee, Faustus, quiet in conceit.

In the last act, Marlowe once more returns us forcefully to the serious business of his play. At the very beginning Wagner is struck by the inconsistency of his master's character. The latter has made his will and hence 'means to die shortly' (V. i. 1). But, says the puzzled servant (5–8):

> if death were nigh
> He would not frolic thus. He's now at supper
> With the scholars, where there's such belly-cheer
> As Wagner in his life ne'er saw the like.

Thus, through the mouth of another character, the playwright shows us Faustus as still the incorrigible hedonist. The Scholars wish him to show them Helen of Troy. Mephistophilis brings in the peerless dame, and the scholars are ravished. The latter leave—and 'Enter an Old Man'. The latter movingly begs Faustus to give up his wicked life (38–63). Here we have explicit statement that Faustus is still a man (and not a spirit); that he still has 'an amiable soul'; that he is still capable of repentance; that if he does not change his wicked ways, his nature will become incapable of contrition; that by 'checking [his] body' 'he may amend [his] soul'. Faustus's reaction to the Old Man's speech is typical. He utterly despairs, is positive of his damnation, and is about to kill himself with a dagger which Mephistophilis provides (63–7). Thus, in the reverse kind of egotism in which Faustus indulges when he is conscience-stricken, he completely misses the burden of the Old Man's message: no man's sins are too great for God to forgive. But the Old Man cries out for him to stop, tells him that 'precious grace' waits only upon prayer for mercy (68–72). Faustus thanks the Old Man for words that 'comfort my distressed soul' and asks to be left alone to ponder his sins (73–5). But the Old Man knows how weak the magician is (76–7):

> Faustus, I leave thee; but with grief of heart,
> Fearing the enemy of thy hapless soul.

We soon see the Old Man was right in his apprehensions. As soon as he has left the stage, Faustus is in the toils (78–81):

> Accursed Faustus, where is mercy now?
> I do repent; and yet I do despair:
> Hell strives with grace for conquest in my breast:
> What shall I do to shun the snares of death?

Hell strives against Heaven: despair against repentance. But as soon as Mephistophilis arrests him for disobedience, commands him to deny God, threatens physical pain—'Or I'll in piecemeal tear thy flesh' (82–4)—the weak-willed voluptuary caves in. He 'repents' (*sic!*) that he has offended Lucifer (85), offers of his own volition to confirm with blood his former vow to Lucifer and does so (86–91), and—characteristically blaming another for his treason—brutally begs Mephistophilis to torture the Old Man 'With greatest torments that our (*sic!*) hell affords' (92–4). Is this the superman whom devotees of the Renaissance paint?

Once more we see the familiar pattern operating. Faustus requests the moly which will deaden his spiritual apprehension (98–104):

> One thing, good servant, let me crave of thee,
> To glut the longing of my heart's desire,—
> That I may have unto my paramour
> That heavenly Helen which I saw of late,
> Whose sweet embraces may extinguish clean
> Those thoughts that do dissuade me from my vow,
> And keep my oath I made to Lucifer.

Helen appears. Faustus delivers the famous apostrophe, 'Was this the face . . .' and leaves the stage with her. How are we to take these lines? The Old Man has appeared in the midst of them and seen and heard Faustus. He recognizes what is happening, and so should we. For the sake of bodily pleasure, Faustus has given up the last possibility of redemption and embraced Hell. We do not even have to recognize that Helen is a succuba, the devil in female guise, to know what Marlowe wants us to know. That there should be no doubt, the Old Man tells us as soon as Faustus and Helen have left the stage together (127–9):

> Accursed Faustus, miserable man,
> That from thy soul exclud'st the grace of Heaven,
> And fliest the throne of his tribunal-seat!

(In the next six lines, Marlowe establishes a strong contrast between the hedonist and the Old Man. The devils come in to torture the latter, but he, strong in his faith, defies their torments.)

The next scene is that of Faustus's going down to Hell (V. 11). The comment of Mephistophilis at its beginning is sharply descriptive (12–16):

> Fond worldling, now his heart-blood dries with grief,
> His conscience kills it and his labouring brain
> Begets a world of idle fantasies,
> To over-reach the Devil; but all in vain,
> His store of pleasures must be sauc'd with pain.

And note how admirably Marlowe shows us the kernel of this unstable, foolish worldling. The Second Scholar has asked him to repent, 'God's mercies are infinite' (40). Faustus replies (41–54):

> But Faustus' offence can ne'er be pardoned: the serpent that tempted Eve may be saved, but not Faustus. O, gentlemen, hear me with patience, and tremble not at my speeches! Though my heart pant and quiver to remember that I have been a student here these thirty years, O, would I had never seen Wittenberg, never read book! and what wonders I have done, all Germany can witness, yea, all the world; for which Faustus hath lost both Germany and the world; yea, heaven itself, heaven, the seat of God, the throne of the blessed, the kingdom of joy; and must remain in hell for ever—hell, oh, hell for ever! Sweet friends, what shall become of Faustus, being in hell for ever!

One should not pass over lightly the exceedingly dramatic nature of this speech. The quaking Faustus is still the blatant egotist. He *knows* that God cannot pardon him! And in the midst of his self-reproach, lo! the basic vanity leaps forth—'and what wonders I have done, all Germany can witness, yea, all the world'. Critics tend to consider Marlowe capable only of broad effects—erroneously, I believe.

Faustus sums up his situation succinctly: 'for the vain pleasure of four and twenty years hath Faustus lost eternal joy and felicity' (67–8). He gave up higher values for lower. And the burden of the

Good and Bad Angels who come on is that for small pleasures the
voluptuary has given up great pleasures, for small pleasures he must
now endure all the horrible sensory tortures of Hell (103–36). The
Bad Angel concludes, 'He that loves pleasure, must for pleasure fall.'
Such is the ironic outcome.

But the most trenchant stroke of Marlowe's pervading irony is in the
famous last soliloquy. Faustus, too late, begs for time to repent, and
in his agony cries out (146), '*O lente, lente currite, noctis equi!*' This
is Ovid, *Amores*, I. xiii. 40. Habituated to sensual pleasure, Faustus—
begging now for time to save his soul—must perforce use the words
of Ovid in his mistress's arms!

My main story is done. I hope I have made my major point, that
the Helen of Troy speech is hardly what critics take it to be, an unen-
cumbered pagan pæan. I hope I have shown that in the pattern of the
play Helen is a temporary pleasure that costs the protagonist eternal
pain. It is worthwhile to examine the lines to Helen more carefully,
for they are fraught with dramatic irony. Faustus himself points out
the danger in Helen's beauty. It caused the great Trojan war—and the
destruction of man's greatest edifices. Faustus's request, 'Sweet Helen,
make me immortal with a kiss', is, of course, blasphemous. On the
contrary, it will mean eternal torment; and it will rob him of immortal
bliss. When he says, 'Her lips suck forth my soul', he is being literally
true. And as he once more kisses her, what an ironic confusion of
values there is!

> Here will I dwell, for heaven is in these lips,
> And all is dross that is not Helena.

Rather, Hell lies in her lips—for the sake of which he has given up
Heaven: and Helen is the 'dross' for which he is giving up the 'all'.
In the rest of the passage, Marlowe's irony persists—but not so near
the surface. There is still a reversal of the normal. Faustus will be
Paris (who was defeated) and fight 'weak Menelaus' (who was stronger
actually). Furthermore, Faustus will be like the violator of order
(Paris), whereas his opponent (the husband, the symbol of order) will
be weak; but in *The Iliad* order wins—and it is bound to win in the
play, too. Faustus will wear the colours of Hell on his crest. He will
ignominiously fight a weak opponent—and he will wound another in
his foot! Helen's beauty is like the night and stars. One remembers:

> Had I as many souls as there be stars,
> I'd give them all for Mephistophilis.   I. iii. 104–5

and

>   as beautiful
> As was bright Lucifer before his fall.   II. i. 155–6

'Brighter art thou than flaming Jupiter' suggests the ever-burning
flames of Hell—of which we hear much in the next scene. And note

the proportion—Helen: Jupiter: : Faustus: 'hapless Semele'. Helen indeed overcomes the hapless Faustus. And note the next proportion —Helen: Jupiter: : Faustus: 'wanton Arethusa'. Wanton Faustus!

From 'Marlowe's *Faustus:* A Reconsideration', in *The Review of English Studies,* vol. XIX, no. 75, 1943, pp. 225–41 (229–41). The text used in this article is that of 1616, see *Dr Faustus: Parallel Texts,* ed. W. W. Greg, Clarendon Press, Oxford, 1950; but the line numbering, etc., is from F. S. Boas's edition, Methuen, London, 1932.

NICHOLAS BROOKE

The Moral Tragedy of *Dr Faustus*

... In *Dr Faustus* ... Marlowe's main pre-occupation ... is still the moral one, of Man's faculties and his voluntary subjection of them to an accepted order. ... It is in the presentation of that theme, then, that we must look, if anywhere, for the consistency of attitude (it will not be more) on which the play's unity should depend. The Play is the thing, but the play is not just 'putting the *Faust Book* on the stage', nor 'exploiting a popular interest in devils and witchcraft'. Marlowe is doing both these things, and both produce their own deviations from a consistent course: but they are not what the Elizabethans would have called the 'cause' of his play. There is a principle of selection in his treatment of the *Faust Book*; and there is an interpretative interest in his handling of witchcraft evident in the (typically Elizabethan) duality of his attitude to the supernatural. On the one hand, supernatural manifestations are external to man; on the other they are partly suggested as objective realizations of psychological conflict: it is not accurate to speak of Mephostophilis solely as the former, any more than it is to speak of the Good and Bad Angels solely as the latter. Whichever they are, psychological or supernatural, their effects and activities must necessarily be the same; but the consistent co-existence of both forms is not necessary and does not take place. That this modifies the idea of individual responsibility which Marlowe develops in the play seems obvious; Faustus is, and is not, in control of the events that destroy him; but Marlowe does not clarify his thought on this matter, and if at one moment he seems clearly to imply one attitude, at another he equally clearly implies the opposite. Mr J. Smith, in an interesting essay[1] which fails to take sufficient account of historical context, avoids this ambiguity by finding allegory at one level only (the psychological) wherever Faustus's moral freedom is tampered with. But this does not seem to be Marlowe's meaning. Faustus attempts to assert his will in opposition to both God and devil and he fails, as it is obvious he must. What is not so obvious is the interpretation Marlowe places on the failure; what significant change of thought caused him to turn from the story of Tamburlaine who even in death can be suggested as triumphant, to Faustus who cannot. The issue has been grossly over-simplified as between atheism and orthodox Christianity; this is particularly dangerous because these terms have changed their common meanings very considerably since the sixteenth century.

The problem, then, is to understand the terms in which Marlowe conceived his drama: to discover whether there does exist a consistency in his attitude to his theme throughout the play to form a sufficient foundation for the patent magnificence of the end. For by the end only is the play widely known, the apostrophe to Helen and Faustus's last speech; but they are sufficient to make it the only Elizabethan play outside Shakespeare that enjoys regular revival at Stratford. For the rest, the play is known to be a wandering, ill-constructed and for the most part ill-written affair. Worse than that, it is erratic in taste and seriousness: it wanders from high philosophical speculation to cheap spectacle and vulgar farce, and offers no clear continuity, no thread of development to which we can relate its flashes of greatness, its hints of profound meaning. The problem is made more difficult by the condition of the text as we have it. Sir Walter Greg[2] has thoroughly worked out the relations of the two early printed texts to Marlowe's own manuscript; the details are controversial, but the main issues are no longer in doubt. *Dr Faustus* was written at the end, not at the beginning, of Marlowe's career; thus any relation of the thought of this play to Marlowe's others must be made on the assumption that it is his last, not his first important statement of his ideas. The 1616 text is the nearer to what Marlowe wrote, and it retains more fully the Morality play features which distinguish *Faustus*. It is precisely this characteristic which seems to have dictated the critical (as opposed to scholarly) preference for the 1604 text which

---

[1] *Scrutiny*, June 1939.
[2] Introduction to his parallel text edition, Oxford, 1950.

persisted until very recently; for the less the 'machinery' was allowed to obtrude, the more easily could the play be represented as a personal tragedy, depending on the character of Faustus himself. Yet Marlowe's drama was never concerned primarily with character—his heroes are not in that sense clearly defined at all: his plays take their source from ideas, and the excitement of their presentation; and his human drama, when it can properly be said to exist, lies again more in predicament than character. It is not the stupidity of Faustus of which we are most aware at the end of the play, but his appalling situation, a man (*any* man) cut off from all contact with humanity, dragged to Hell for eternity and seeing visions of Heaven as he goes. The situation depends on the Morality of the play, and to cut that out is to cut out the foundations of the tragedy. The deficiencies of the 1604 text seem to be, as Greg suggests, caused by a need for easy theatrical effect and simple staging in the provinces; it therefore reduces not only the Morality framework (which might not be 'good theatre') but also such spectacular (and surely Marlovian) effects as the presence of the Princes of Hell overlooking the last scene; as well as making the most of opportunities for farce even at the expense of serious intent.

The deficiencies which Greg notices in the 1616 text may also, I suspect, have an important bearing on critical interpretation. Where his manuscript was damaged, the editor was forced to rely on the printed version, and further (the last infernal bar to the present inquiry) he found it necessary to tone the play down to conform with the more rigorous censorship of blasphemy. In such obvious cases as the substitution of 'Dear Heaven' for 'My God, My God', the earlier text supplies the stronger line: but I shall try to show that Marlowe's fundamental ideas in this play were blasphemous—circumspectly so, no doubt, in the first place (blasphemy was always a serious offence; Marlowe was awaiting trial for it when he was murdered)—but where they showed a little too plain, the lines may have been re-written by the editor in just those contexts of moral argument which were omitted from the 1604 text. Such a possibility (as it is based on mere conjecture) need not be taken very seriously, but it emphasizes the kind of obscurity we find in the play.

Clearly then, the first point to be faced about *Dr Faustus* is that it is in construction a Morality play. This is the burthen of recent criticism, notably by Professor Kirschbaum[3] and Dr Greg[4] who have independently arrived at remarkably similar conclusions. Professor Kirschbaum insists that we must forget what we would like the play to be (a tragedy) and concentrate on what it is, a morality. He insists that the prologue must be taken literally, when it announces the play as a spectacle of the clever fellow who excels in learning

[3] In *Review of English Studies*, July 1943.
[4] In *Modern Language Review*, April 1946.

> Till, swollen with the cunning of a self-conceit,
> His waxen wings did mount above his reach,
> And melting, heavens conspired his overthrow.
>
> *Prologue*; 20–2—Greg's conjectural reconstruction

In other words, the fate of the presumptuous Icarus, the Christian moral of humility and denial of self in the presence of God. On that plane the play continues: Faustus is visited periodically by a Good and a Bad Angel who makes obvious suggestions, he is warned finally by a pious and saintly Old Man, comes to a deservedly 'sticky end', and the appropriate comment is in the epilogue:

> Cut is the branch that might have grown full straight, . . .
> Faustus is gone: regard his hellish fall, . . .   *Epilogue*; 1 & 4

It is always tempting in dramatic criticism to appeal against over-subtlety and ingenuity, and to claim full attention only for what is made obvious. That is what Kirschbaum does, and if he is right we must accept the idea of Marlowe intending to write a simple Morality Play of a kind frequent in the sixteenth century. The curious thing about this is that it flatly contradicts older views as to the central interest of the play: tending to undervalue or completely ignore the Morality features, critics thought of Dr Faustus as a kind of Renaissance superman condemned to tragic failure; a man who expresses superbly a longing for knowledge, beauty, wealth and power. The opening scene supports this view, with Faustus examining all the established lines of human knowledge and finding them all inadequate, too limited; the aim he sets himself is achievement of the supreme desire of Man:

> Oh, what a world of profit and delight,
> Of power, of honour, of omnipotence
> Is promised to the studious artizan!   I. i. 51–3

And these he pursues—begging Mephostophilis for information, recounting how he has made Blind Homer sing to him, and the chorus tells of his journey through the air to see the astronomical system in its entirety, and still at the end he pursues perfect physical beauty in Helen. All the great passages of the play are concerned with these notions, and they are the only positive ideas advanced: it is impossible to come away from seeing or reading it without having the magnificence of Faustus's visions uppermost in the mind. The final moral exhortation not to practise more than heavenly power permits is either forgotten, or leaves a stale and dusty taste behind it.

Kirschbaum and Greg both recognize this difficulty and seek to overcome it by postulating a gradual deterioration of Faustus's character throughout the play from noble-mindedness to mere depravity. And there, they suggest, the tragedy lies: in pursuing physical pleasure, Faustus neglects spiritual values, and deteriorates to such a weakness of will that he cannot assert himself against the temptations of the devil even when the penalty is near at hand.

There are three vital reasons why I do not think this is a satisfactory view. First of all, this gradual deterioration of character does not seem to be in the play: it is foisting an idea of drama and behaviour on to Marlowe which is wholly unlike him, wholly foreign to the kind of play he and his contemporaries were composing. Faustus is certainly sometimes coarse and trivial—but no more so at the end than at the beginning of the play: in the first scene, he repeats his aims more vulgarly, or rather mixing the noble constantly with the trivial:

> Shall I make spirits fetch me what I please,
> Resolve me of all ambiguities,
> Perform what desperate enterprise I will?
> I'll have them fly to India for gold,
> Ransack the ocean for orient pearl,
> And search all corners of the new-found world
> For pleasant fruits and princely delicates.
> I'll have them read me strange philosophy
> And tell the secrets of all foreign kings;   I. i. 77–85

and so on: Faustus's pursuits are like this throughout the play; at one moment strange philosophy, at the next mere secrets of all foreign kings. Similarly there is a mixture of serious thought and cheap iconoclasm in Faustus's well-known rejection of the sciences, and it is followed (still in the first scene) by the less popular lines

> Philosophy is odious and obscure,
> Both law and physic are for petty wits,
> Divinity is basest of the three,
> Unpleasant, harsh, contemptible and vild;   I. i. 104–7

So Faustus oscillates throughout the play, turning from the nature of Hell to demanding a wife; from Blind Homer to delight in the farcical seven deadly sins. I can see no steady deterioration in all this: there is less serious thought perhaps at the end, but not much less: Faustus asks for Helen not philosophy, but he states as early as Act II Scene ii that it is Pleasure he is after with Homer, Alexander and Œnone, and he repeats it in Act III Scene i:

> Whilst I am here on earth let me be cloyed
> With all things that delight the heart of man.   III. i. 59–60

That is immediately after the chorus tells of his journey to find the secrets of astronomy, and at the end of the play it is for his prodigious learning that his students remember Faustus the sorcerer. The fact is that *we* make a distinction between Knowledge and Pleasure which is foreign to Marlowe: the philosophy of *Faustus*, like that of *Tamburlaine*, is primarily hedonistic; the man has appetites, and his pleasure is to satisfy them. He has an appetite for knowledge, and another for sex; both are extreme, for complete knowledge and for perfect sex; but the only qualitative distinction is between completeness and incompleteness. If Faustus had deteriorated in character during the play he would be content with any 'hot whore', not insist on Helen herself.

This seems to me the second vital objection to their theory, and to get over it both Greg and Kirschbaum suppose the apostrophe to Helen to be ironic: they remind us that Helen is only a devil in disguise, the same spirit that Faustus produced to beguile his students' senses; and further that in committing adultery with the devil (as we are given to understand that he does) Faustus commits the final sin, consummates his bond with Lucifer, and from then on is acknowledged even by the Good Angel to be beyond redemption. This is all true, but it does not make the Helen episode ironic: if it were, the actor would be asked to deliver a supremely persuasive erotic speech to convince his audience of the value of Pleasure in the face of their foreknowledge that Helen is only a spirit—and yet, deliberately fail to persuade them. An unlikely performance. To assert irony in a passage where the words never suggest it, where the tone is of exultant satisfaction, is to ignore the nature of the poetic statement: here, as elsewhere in the play, Marlowe has put conviction into the voice of Hell, not of Heaven. Certainly there is irony in this, but it is not of the kind Kirschbaum and Greg suggest, degrading Faustus's 'weak sensuality' as a cause of his abandoning lasting pleasure for the sake of temporary.

What emerges then, once the Morality framework is acknowledged, is the very odd state of affairs that all the positive statements of the play, supported by the finest verse, are against the declared Christian moral. The pleasures Faustus wants are made clear to the mind and the imagination. To the mind they are, as usual with Marlowe, made disconcertingly clear: the mingling of strange philosophy with the secrets of all foreign kings is reminiscent of Tamburlaine's famous speech:

> Our souls, whose faculties can comprehend
> The wondrous architecture of the world . . .
> Still climbing after knowledge infinite . . .
> Until we reach the ripest fruit of all,
> That perfect bliss and sole felicity,
> The sweet fruition of an earthly crown.
>
> II. vii. 21–9—ed. Ellis-Fermor

To Marlowe these apparently odd juxtapositions are not ironic: I said before that he does not make qualitative distinctions; what the human mind desires, it desires, and an odd assortment is the inevitable result. His imagination fired at the crown or at Machiavellian politics, for the power of individual expansion they permit; but it fired at other less reputable occupations, such as his employment as a spy which many connect with his curiosity about the secrets of all foreign kings—for even in that there is a sense of power.

These positive 'evils' which Faustus wants are made abundantly clear then to the mind; there is no need to stress the imaginative quality of the Helen speech, or of the first turn to magic:

> emperors and kings
> Are but obeyed in their several provinces,
> Nor can they raise the wind or rend the clouds;
> But his dominion that excells in this
> Stretcheth as far as doth the mind of man:
> A sound magician is a demi-god;
> Here tire my braines to get a deity!   I. i. 55–61

But for the opposite, the Christian virtue and the hope of Heaven, which Greg and Kirschbaum would have us believe Marlowe is trying to recommend, not only is the imagination scarcely given a chance to be fired by them, they are never made in the least clear to the mind. From the dull and feeble bleatings of the Good Angel at the beginning, to the conventional phrases of the Old Man and the Epilogue, all statements of the 'good' moral remain vague, flat, meaningless.

The interpretation of the play as deliberately invoking Christian ideals is therefore as unsatisfactory as the older view of the tragedy of aspiring man. Neither can be dismissed, neither is anything like a complete view of *Dr Faustus*. It is not possible to believe that Marlowe intended a sound Christian play but unconsciously emphasized the wrong moral: the nature of the evidence I have examined would make such large demands on Marlowe's unconscious as to amount to insanity. I therefore conclude, that Marlowe chose deliberately to use the Morality form, and to use it perversely, to invert or at least to satirize its normal intention. To understand the significance of this, we must imagine the position of a playwright in 1591 or 1592 when Marlowe was writing *Faustus:* old morality plays were still performed, and some of them may not have been very old; but much as the leading playwrights owed to the Morality tradition, they did not write simple Morality plays such as *Faustus* purports to be. The comedies of Lyly and Greene, the tragedies of Kyd, and Marlowe's other plays, have moved a long way from puppet-manipulation of abstractions, and even *Gorboduc* thirty years earlier had called its Good and Bad Angels by the names of political advisers. Abstractions appeared in popular plays much later than that, but by 1590 the full apparatus of Morality was an old and musty form of drama, as in their turn were Marlowe's own plays by 1600. For Marlowe to write such a play at such a time therefore suggests satire: it is the least likely way for him to have chosen to express a volte-face from near-atheism of opinion, and

violent anti-Christian satire in *Tamburlaine* and *The Jew of Malta*
to orthodox Christian belief. I believe that Marlowe's adoption of
Morality form must be seen as a deliberate mis-use of popular old-
fashioned material.

There are two possible forms this mis-use might have taken: firstly,
to present Faustus as a simple Morality story, and to give it a bitter
ironic twist right through. In this case, there could be no sustained
elaboration of the opposite notion of morality ironically implied, nor
could the death of the hero unrepentant be anything but a somewhat
nasty joke: it offers no course of deliberate action to Faustus to enable
us to understand the state of his mind in his last, wholly tragic speech.
The predicament would be simply that of a silly old man paying the
price of his stupidity—and there is in that nothing of the mental
conflict, the doubt and terror that Marlowe expresses. The other
possible mis-use of the Morality form is to invert it completely, to
portray the search of a man for Hell not Heaven, to assert constantly
the idea that everything is upside down, that so called evil is in fact
good, that the struggle of Faustus is to be anti-Christ, not Christian. . . .

It seems to me clear that Marlowe was not strictly an atheist at all:
that is to say, he never expressly denies the existence of God, not even
in the wild blasphemies Baines collected for his indictment. I should
doubt very much whether such a complete denial of the idea of an
almighty God was possible within the mental horizon of even an
advanced thinker of the 1590s;[5] I am certain that it was far from
Marlowe's mind. The 'atheism' for which he should have stood his
trial, and which he hints at throughout his plays, was not atheism at all,
but blasphemy, a repeated protest against the nature of God implied
in His treatment of Man, a protest whose bitterness implies acceptance of the *existence* of God. It is for that reason that Marlowe persistently invokes the idea of a jealous God, one who could bear no brother
near the throne. The dramatic tension of the Faustus story as Marlowe
presents it lies primarily in the fact that Faustus is determined to
satisfy the demands of his nature as God has made him—to be himself
a deity—and that is forbidden: it can only be achieved by a conscious
rejection of the God who created him in his own image, but denied
him (as much as Lucifer) fulfilment of that image. . . .

The idea of 'reach' is at once the theme of Act I Scene i, in Faustus's
rejection of the sciences, his search for greater opportunity and his
adoption of magic:

> But his dominion that excells in this
> Stretcheth as far as doth the mind of man:

and beyond that into explicit challenge of his aim:

---

[5] A few years later Tourneur uses the word in a strict sense in *The Atheist's
Tragedy;* but as a fascinating speculative outrage.

> A sound magician is a demi-god;
> Here tire my braines to get a deity!   I. i. 58–61

The angels appear, and as their remarks well illustrate the theological bias I have remarked, I shall quote them in full. The Good Angel opposes Faustus's aspirations only with negatives, the idea of a God of wrath and the ironic suggestion that he should read the scriptures whose inadequacy he has just asserted:

> O Faustus, lay that damned book aside
> And gaze not on it lest it tempt thy soul
> And heap God's heavy wrath upon thy head.
> Read, read the scriptures; that is blasphemy.

Whereas the Bad Angel repeats Faustus's own conception:

> Go forward Faustus, in that famous art
> Wherein all nature's treasury is contained:
> Be thou on earth as Jove is in the sky,
> Lord and commander of these elements.   I. i. 68–75

Faustus therefore invites the aid of Valdes and Cornelius, well-known as magicians, whose dominion does not stretch anything like as far as doth the mind of man, for all their skill: this is an important point, we are made aware that magic does nothing in itself, that it is only an instrument through which Faustus's own peculiar potentiality for greatness may operate. In this sense, Marlowe's treatment of magic is comparable to his treatment of Senecan or Machiavellian ideas of princecraft: in each case what he knew to be 'evil' in any accepted sense, he invoked deliberately as a means for the individual to surmount the restrictions of social morality, to realize his potentiality for supreme power: Tamburlaine, Barabbas, and Faustus all have this in common, a vision of greatness denied by the Laws to which ordinary men are subjected; and they seek freedom by being a king above the Law[6], by employing an infinity of obscure cunning, and lastly for the widest freedom of all, Magic. In each case, Marlowe's conception is aided by opportunities for stage spectacle which seems to have been as much to his taste as his audience's: in *Tamburlaine,* Royal pageantry and colourful and bloody displays of sovereignty; in *The Jew of Malta* sinister trickery, poisons, and vats of boiling oil; in *Faustus,* fireworks, conjuring tricks and scenes of Heaven and Hell. He delighted not only in the philosophical implications of Faustus's act, but also in all the details of the Black Art in which he was widely read.[7]

Up to a point this mixture of the serious and the silly relates to what I have already said about Marlowe's philosophical position; but it

---

[6] See A. P. Rossiter: *English Drama from early time to the Elizabethans*, pp. 157–9.

[7] See Paul H. Kocher in *Modern Philology*, August 1940.

relates also to the popular dramatic tradition in which he was writing, and more particularly to the Morality plays whose form he was deliberately reviving. For the most astonishing thing to a modern reader of the Moralities is commonly how much gross *im*morality they include: that the vices have more than their fair share of the entertainment and constantly figure as genuinely entertaining rogues without whom the moralizing would be intolerable. For that reason they frequently unbalance the morals by seductive burlesque, leaving us in doubt whether the serious is so serious, whether the whole matter is after all an uproarious fa..e. This ambivalent outlook, as A. P. Rossiter insists, is a recurrent one from the middle ages to Shakespeare, leaving our school-tidy minds bewildered by a constant equivocation about the one thing of which the plays ought to be certain, until we are jolted into acknowledging that there is in this a disturbing but very real life-likeness.

With this tradition in mind, it is possible to understand something of the horseplay to which Faustus himself descends, and certainly those farcical scenes whose crudity causes so much discussion. In a 'good' morality, the clowns burlesque the virtues presented, but end 'in the mud' as they should, while the virtues triumph. In Faustus it is the 'bad' hero who is burlesqued by Wagner and the clowns, and the impact of their activities on the main theme must be observed. Wretchedly written their scenes may be, but if Marlowe did not actually write them, he planned their existence and they are in any case little more than plans—plans for a slapstick performance by antic clowns of the circus variety, for whom good words would be unnecessary, as well as probably wasted.

Act I Scene ii immediately reveals Wagner as a mocking comic, teasing the scholars by withholding and then giving casually the sensational news that his master is dining with the magicians, which he ends with the equivocal (and naughty) remark: 'and so, the Lord bless you, preserve you, and keep you, my dear brethren' (I. ii. 25–7). The scholars also give a different angle on Faustus's action, referring to Valdes and Cornelius as infamous throughout the world, seeing his friendship with them as damnable merely, bereft of all the splendour Faustus had given it.

Damnable it is meant to be, and in the next scene Faustus reveals his full consciousness of the fact, as he performs the rites of conjuration. Amongst the manuals of the Black Art available to Marlowe, the details of raising devils vary considerably, but the basic method remains always the same—the acts of worship of God are to be inverted, the consecration of devotion has to be turned into an elaborate rite of desecration. In some rites, there are protective measures to be taken, making the conjuring more of an experiment than a final act.[8]

[8] See E. M. Butler: *Ritual Magic.*

Faustus might mean that, when after listing the things he has done, he says:

> Then fear not, Faustus, to be resolute
> And try the uttermost magic can perform.   I. iii. 14–15

But it appears rather that he is afraid of making a mistake which would give the devil power over him instead of vice versa. This idea of resolution is always demanded of witches, and Valdes and Cornelius had stressed it: with Faustus it becomes a vital refrain, 'Faustus, be resolute', in all his dealings with the devil. Its constant re-iteration throughout the play and even in the last scene calls attention to a point which seems to be constantly overlooked: Faustus is always afraid not of the inevitable end of his twenty-four years, but of some immediate failure, the result of irresolution; of the threat the Bad Angel makes in Act II Scene ii: 'If thou repent, devils will tear thee in pieces.' On the purely theatrical aspect of Faustus's dealings in magic, then, it is not a simple question of getting power for twenty-four years at the cost of eternal damnation: Faustus gains his power at the cost of perpetual danger.

At that level, Faustus's activities do not necessarily extend beyond the commonplace wickedness envisaged by the students. But when Mephostophilis has been triumphantly produced (and bullied into a change of costume) the tone changes to intellectual seriousness, to a discussion of the real relationship of Faustus and his devil:

> *Faust.*   Did not my conjuring speeches raise thee? Speak.
> *Meph.*   That was the cause, but yet *per accidens*:
> For when we hear one rack the name of God,
> Abjure the scriptures and his saviour Christ,
> We fly in hope to get his glorious soul;
> Nor will we come unless he use such means
> Whereby he is in danger to be damned.
> Therefore the shortest cut for conjuring
> Is stoutly to abjure the Trinity
> And pray devoutly to the prince of hell.   I. iii. 45–54

Marlowe turns the cheap indignity of Hell at once into a conception of Mephostophilis as a voluntary agent, not a vulgar slave. And from that emerges the famous definition of Hell:

> Why this is hell, nor am I out of it.
> Thinkst thou that I, who saw the face of God
> And tasted the eternal joys of heaven,
> Am not tormented with ten thousand hells
> In being deprived of everlasting bliss?
> O Faustus, leave these frivolous demands,
> Which strike a terror to my fainting soul.   I. iii. 76–81

This is the one passage of imaginative suggestion of Heaven, and it comes from the devil. Faustus contemptuously rejects it:

> What, is great Mephostophilis so passionate
> For being deprivèd of the joys of heaven?
> Learn thou of Faustus manly fortitude
> And scorn those joys thou never shalt possess.   I. iii. 82–5

Again Faustus repeats the idea of resolution—'manly fortitude'—but in a different context, of philosophical discussion not mere theatrical magic: in this latter part of the scene, Faustus's act is reconsidered in terms of its more profound significance. The direct negation of God is not here simply a magic formula, it is an act of Will on Faustus's part, asserted in pursuit of an idea of good in direct contradiction to the Christian idea. In this scene and constantly throughout the play (despite some commonplace insinuations by the Bad Angel at the end) Faustus is not subjected to any simple 'temptation' of the ordinary Morality kind. . . . He is in danger of persecution at the beginning from nothing but his own sense of frustration. It can be argued that this is only a subtle form of temptation, but for the present purpose that is a sophistication: about succcumbing to temptation there is necessarily a negative suggestion, of failure of the Will; Faustus's self-damnation is wholly positive, achieved by an assertion not a failure of his Will. And it is of feebleness that he accuses Mephostophilis. Just as Marlowe has shown Mephostophilis to enjoy the dignity of free will, so Faustus is to be seen as choosing voluntarily, with knowledge of all that it means, Hell instead of Heaven. That is why I say that Marlowe has inverted the Morality structure: the course of Faustus's resolution is to damn himself; his temptation, his weakness, is in offers of repentance. Faustus's Hell is not at first a place of torture, it is Hell only in that it is absence of Heaven, it is an extreme of anti-God whose nature is deliberately opposed to the Angels' joyous submission to the service of the Omnipotent. Heaven is the subjection of self, Hell in this sense is the assertion of self. As I have already said, the foundation of Marlowe's philosophical position is that man has certain over-riding desires whose realization is denied by any form of servitude, and the order of God is, as Milton's Satan observed, an order of servitude.

Marlowe is not, of course, propounding a practicable idea of how men should live (he does not envisage a race of Nietzschean or even Shavian supermen), he is discussing the nature of Man in relation to the God that made him in his own image, with an urge to be like his maker, omnipotent. Hence the sin of Lucifer prince of Hell although technically orthodox—Pride—is given an odd twist by Mephostophilis' statement of it:

> Oh, by aspiring pride and insolence,
> For which God threw him from the face of heaven.   I. iii. 67–8

The ironic tone gives the lines a strange prominence: Lucifer was expelled for precisely the attitude Faustus is now adopting, but expelled (in these lines) by an irritated and petulant God. The idea of the deity which Marlowe suggests here (and elsewhere) is simply of a successful Lucifer or Faustus, one who has the absolute degree of magnificence, and cannot bear to have it dimmed by a rival. That there is another idea of God (or perhaps another, more humble, view of man) is insisted at once in the wholly different tone of Mephostophilis's next words. But for Faustus's attitude here, we must understand not only the hint of a jealous God, but of a particular kind of jealousy.

A favourite Renaissance source for ideas on secular virtue was Aristotle's *Ethics*. The conception, for instance, of Tudor king or Italian prince was compared to Aristotle's description of the Magnificent Man, or even of the μεγαλωψυχος, the Great-souled Man; he who excels in all worldly 'goods', wealth, dignity, popularity and so on, who is a great patron of the arts, and who is superior to all the limitations of lesser men. But two important aspects of the Great-souled man Aristotle stresses: first, that he must be wholly resolute in his pursuit of greatness, that the slightest hesitation or weakness is alien to his nature: 'For the great-souled man is justified in despising other people—his estimates are correct.'[9] And secondly, that he will tolerate no rival within his sphere of influence who might dim his glory: 'he will not go where other people take the first place' and 'he will be incapable of living at the will of another, since to do so is slavish'. It is not of course necessary to suppose that Marlowe devised his version of these ideas direct from Aristotle, but his years at Cambridge could hardly have been passed without reading the Greek.[10] At any rate, an understanding of Aristotle greatly illuminates what it is that Faustus is trying to achieve: the subjective aim of self-expansion is equated with the objective ideal of Aristotelian greatness, and not only are God and Lucifer treated as rival magnificos, but Faustus himself is aiming at that state. That is the philosophical reason for his fear of failure. If he weakens, he will be shown to be less-than-great-souled, he will have failed to gain his deity and will lay himself open to the punishment of God and the revenge of Lucifer, and be torn to pieces. In inverting the Morality pattern of rewards in Heaven and punishments in Hell, Marlowe (as I said before) does not simply reverse this: Heaven is not a punishment, nor is it a reward; it is a wholly different ethos, an idea of humble service which Faustus rejects as unworthy of his nature. Rewards and punishments have therefore both to be in Hell. Hell is used in a number of senses during the play, at a number of different levels, but the central ambiguity is I think between these two: the Hell Faustus seeks, which represents to him the free range of his Will to resolve to be what he thinks it is in his nature to be; and on the other hand the more familiar Hell of

---

[9] *Nichomachean Ethics*, IV, iii.
[10] See B. Tapper in *Studies in Philology*, April 1930.

the Middle Ages, of unspeakable devils, tortures and indignity, which
serves to represent Faustus's fear of failure.

These ideas are hinted in Act I Scene iii, and are developed in the
second act; but in between there is a piece of clownage, Wagner
directly burlesquing his master, raising devils, arrogating to himself
the title of 'Master' and making a slave of the clown with a gibberish
of pseudo-learning and Latin: the ironic suggestions in this of over-
weening and ridicule are developed later.

Act II develops to the full the tragic drama, Faustus's mental
conflict, his waverings and his sudden moves forward into devilry. He
starts alone in his study, triumphantly asserting his damnation:

> Now, Faustus, must thou needs be damned,
>   canst not be saved!
> What boots it then to think of God or heaven?
> Away with such vain fancies, and despair;
> Despair in God and trust in Beelzebub.   II. i. 1–4

Nevertheless, as those lines ironically imply, Faustus is not so resolute
—something soundeth in his ears—and he has to drive himself back
by re-iteration of his basic intention as I see it:

> To God! He loves thee not:
> The god thou servest is thine own appetite.   II. i. 9–10

from which he builds up to a typically Marlovian brutal hyperbole:

> And offer lukewarm blood of new-born babes.

The angels add nothing new, except that the suggestion of wealth
fires Faustus's imagination and enables him to be resolute again and
call Mephostophilis. Already in Act I there is a suggestion of irony in
Faustus's vaunting refusal to believe Mephostophilis on his own
torment; here that suggestion becomes more marked. Mephostophilis
promises to be his slave.

> And give thee more than thou hast wit to ask.   II. i. 45

Faustus is suddenly suggested to be incapable of what he aims at—but
Mephostophilis reassures him by offering him again what he wants:

> And then be thou as great as Lucifer.   II. i. 50

The signing of the bond gives Faustus another moment of panic, but
the knowledge of his remoteness from Heaven spurs him on to resolution in his dealings with Hell. With the bond signed, the deed done,
Faustus becomes more blatantly confident; Mephostophilis defines the
situation again:

> All places shall be hell that is not heaven.   II. i. 124

And Faustus retorts 'I think hell's a fable', and proceeds ebulliently to stress the idea that Hell is a mental state, and that an after-life of physical torture is nothing but 'trifles and mere old wives' tales'. With that he turns aside to the lively interchange about wives and whores and turns again to end the scene by accepting the Book of Knowledge.

Greg conjectures plausibly that there should follow a comic scene here: it would in fact make a better place for an interval in modern performance than the usual act division, as Act II Scene i should obviously follow at once both as a climax and an illumination of what has gone before. Scene ii demands an interval of time, and opens with a new doubt in Faustus's mind, another offer to repent. Mephostophilis counters it with a syllogism:

> But thinkst thou heaven is such a glorious thing?
> I tell thee, Faustus, it is not half so fair
> As thou or any man that breathes on earth.
> *Faust.* How provst thou that?
> *Meph.* 'Twas made for man; then he's more excellent.

Which Faustus answers with another syllogism:

> If heaven was made for man, 'twas made for me.   II. ii. 5–10

It is hard to know exactly how to take these lines—our immediate reaction is to dismiss Mephostophilis's statement as obviously false logic; on the other hand it is of a kind with Faustus's own arguments at the opening of the play, and with Marlowe's statements elsewhere. At any rate, it leads to Faustus's determination to renounce this magic and repent, which immediately recalls the Angels. Here it is apparent that the drama of Faustus's soul has advanced: the deed of self-damnation is done, and his mind twists in terror towards an easy if ignoble salvation more tempting now that it is impossible. The Good Angel does tempt him now: '*yet* God will pity thee', but the Bad Angel retorts at once 'Thou art a spirit; God cannot pity thee.' (II. ii. 12–13). Greg points the force of this line when he remarks that here and always in the play, 'spirit' is used in a strict sense, meaning devil. Faustus despairs and talks of suicide but recalls his Will by contemplation of Blind Homer, of Alexander's love and Œnone's death: his consolation is in voluptuous pleasure certainly, but it is not the degrading sensuality it has been called; it is Faustus's god of Appetite which turns him back to his purpose

> I am resolved Faustus shall not repent.   II. ii. 31

He turns back to Astronomy, and the irony again asserts itself: in the first place, there is Marlowe's dilemma that he cannot display more knowledge than man possessed; but secondly, Faustus is cheated in his bond: Mephostophilis refuses to state who made the world. Faustus's attempt may be magnificent, to gain a deity, but the terrible fact remains that God is God: the challenge is not atheism, it is against the monstrous nature of a world where man is created to want to be at his finest precisely what he is not allowed to be; the God is the God of Milton's Satan—'equald in intellect, but supream in force'.

Again Faustus tries to repent, and again the Angels appear, to stress now more obviously the cruder physical nature of Faustus's predicament, the 'machinery' of Heaven and Hell:

> *Bad* If thou repent, devils will tear thee in pieces.
> *Good* Repent, and they shall never raze thy skin.   II. ii. 82–3

Faustus, for the only time before the end, does repent, and calls on Christ to save him. It is the supreme weakening which offers Lucifer the chance to throw Faustus straight down from his attempted magnificence, it is a direct transgression of the bond. As at the end, the mention of Christ brings the prince of Hell straight to Faustus, now only to warn him. The presence of the Stygian Trinity restores his confidence and he renews his vows. But our awareness of his weakness, of his failure to be resolute is accentuated in the farce that follows. The Seven Deadly Sins are presented as a grotesque parody of Faustus's god of Appetite. All his voluptuous aspirations are turned to vulgarity. Pride is mere disdain, Covetousness is gold locked up, and so on—for each sin, the worst is futility, Faustus's means to magnificence degraded to ends in themselves with a sterility set in bawdy farce. His comment on it is typically equivocal:

> Oh, how this sight doth delight my soul!   II. ii. 167

That burlesque is followed by another, the clowns again, conjuring, shown as able to imagine no greater good to use their devils for, than to get wine enough to be drunk. The same point had been made in the last clowning scene (I. iv), where the clown falls a ready victim to Wagner's wit:

> The villain's out of service, and so hungry that I know he would give his soul to the devil for a shoulder of mutton, though it were blood-raw.
> *Clo.* Not so, neither; I had need to have it well roasted, and good sauce to it, if I pay so dear, I can tell you.   I. iv. 8–12

Wagner has his man: base mortals cannot will enough to use magic profitably. In this early scene the impact is in doubt: it either hints that Faustus is superior to ordinary mortals, or that he like them in a higher range, is also condemned to littleness, far from the aim he sets. By the end of the second act, this latter insinuation must necessarily prevail. God's revenge comes before the end of the play, in the ever clearer ironic implication that He has kept man from deity by restricting his ability: has given him the imagination to desire greatness, but not the Will to achieve it. The urgency of the drama of Faustus lies in the protest against this inevitable torture for God's creature, man.

If that *is* the constitution of the world, then this indeed is Hell, nor are we out of it, and Life is precisely the mixture of tragically doomed yet magnificent effort with mere mocking farce, that Marlowe makes his play.

The tragic concept of the play, then, is fully presented by the end of Act II: Acts III and IV detail Faustus's achievements, his twenty-four years of power after Lucifer has left him to enjoy it. They are unquestionably disappointing acts: in serious passages they lack either the tragic splendour or the intellectual insight of the scenes I have been discussing; when they turn to farce the critical comment is less biting, the sting is gone. Yet however feebly worked out it may be, the plan of the play continues intelligibly: the devil's agent provides Faustus with all he wants: knowledge, power, wealth—success in every direction, but always cheated of the supreme success, the consciousness of absolute greatness. It is absurd to pretend that these acts represent a lowering of standard in Faustus's achievement, because for so long he trifles with vulgarity in Rome, or mere conjuring tricks in Germany; but they do reveal clearly the persistent weakness in Marlowe's work. A. P. Rossiter remarks that '[Kyd] is a true dramatist in his plotting; Marlowe, except in Edward II, is a dramatist only in his dramatic poetry—in great vistas of *mind,* rather than of the slipknot of fate or events pulling tight on human lives.'[11] This suggests the fault of these acts: the story of Faustus's fame on earth has to be told, but its telling presents a dramatic problem which Marlowe has failed to solve. I have already said that it is impossible to show Faustus acquiring complete knowledge of the universe, for the obvious reason that Marlowe didn't possess it himself; so he simply states that Faustus did achieve it in two fine choruses and leaves the action to what can be shown, the power of human interference. The result is such a complete lack of balance, that the subject matter of the choruses is often forgotten, and Faustus accused of mere triviality in these scenes. The failure to invent a satisfactory organization for this matter apparently had its effect on Marlowe's writing; whether he actually wrote the scenes himself, or whether (as is usually argued, most recently by Sir Walter Greg) he left the major part of their composition to a collaborator, the conclusion is the same: that he was bored by them, and expended little effort or imaginative power on them. But Greg does not doubt that Marlowe planned them, and therefore their action and general significance are his responsibility.

The Chorus before Act III tells of Faustus's journey through the air, his discovery of all the secrets of astronomy; he is now turning to cosmography. And Act III Scene i shows him at it, attending to a long lecture on the sights of Rome in which Mephostophilis plays the part of a Renaissance Baedeker. . . .

---

[11] Op. cit. p. 160.

Act IV returns to Germany, to present Faustus at last as renowned for knowledge and power as he wished, admired by his emperor and his fellow citizens and demonstrating his talents in a series of tricks and jokes which again end in clownage, literally in horseplay. Once indeed, Faustus comes out from this to make an explicit statement of his frustration and despair, but the lines are neither impressive nor revealing (IV. v. 21–6).

With the opening of Act V (for which no chorus is needed) the wheel has gone full circle: Faustus is back at Wittenberg with his students, and as the twenty-four years draw to their end, the full drama reasserts itself. Faustus's last effort at achieving admiration, is to offer his scholars anything they please; they choose—and Marlowe offers no suggestion of unscholarly inappropriateness—they choose to see Helen of Troy. With the entry of the Old Man, despair returns and Faustus's tragic dilemma takes on an extra dimension: it is here that it becomes most vitally important not to over-simplify the drama of ideas, the vista of mind, if the meaning as well as the mood of the final tragedy is to be understood. The Old Man asserts at length a Christian criticism of Faustus's behaviour: a dichotomy of soul and body that Faustus has never admitted. Commenting on the raising of Helen, he says:

> Though thou hast now offended like a man,
> Do not persever in it like a devil.
> Yet, yet, thou hast an amiable soul
> If sin by custom grow not into nature.   V. i. 40–3

Faustus does not comment on this argument, but consciousness of his own failure causes him in panic to turn to the Old Man's offer of mercy, of resignation to a power greater than himself. The Old Man has implied that there is still hope, that irretrievable damnation (represented by Helen, the supreme satisfaction of the appetite for beauty) has not yet been achieved. Faustus is torn between despair equals repentance, and despair equals acknowledgement of Hell triumphant:

> I do repent, and yet I do despair:
> Hell strives with grace for conquest in my breast.   V. i. 70–1

But the peculiar predicament which I have stressed and which the Old Man, representing orthodox Christianity, ignores, is at once brought out with the appearance of Mephostophilis: the morality is still inverted, there are still rewards and punishments in Faustus's Hell:

> Thou traitor Faustus, I arrest thy soul
> For disobedience to my sovereign lord:
> Revolt, or I'll in piecemeal tear thy flesh.   V. i. 73–5

And for the last time, Faustus revolts, expressly renews his bond with

Lucifer, and makes his final exertion of resolution for his scholars' choice, Helen of Troy.

> One thing, good servant, let me crave of thee
> To glut the longing of my heart's desire;
> That I may have unto my paramour
> That heavenly Helen which I saw of late,
> Whose sweet embracings may extinguish clear
> Those thoughts that do dissuade me from my vow,
> And keep the oath I made to Lucifer.   V. i. 89–95

Faustus's sin has been carried to the point at which he must make a final choice between Heaven and Hell, and he makes it deliberately for Hell, as the Old Man (who watches him make love to Helen) clearly states. But they see the act in different lights: to the Old Man, Helen is the supreme temptation; to Faustus she is the supreme expression of the appetitive Will. In choosing her he commits his final negation of the idea of service to a God, to the whole Elizabethan conception of the proper relation of appetite to intellect, of right order. Faustus's appeal to Helen is primarily moral, not an aesthetic escape from the moral. Nine-tenths of his consciousness is fear and failure; reason and experience deny the validity of his appetitive Will, but at the last it is not to reason and humility he resorts, not even to that that his scholars invite him, but to Helen. Never before in the play does Marlowe make the opposition so explicit; the Old Man's theological conception of coition with the devil as the unforgivable sin, is shadowy; Faustus makes the climax of his fortunes a moral assertion beside which the theological looks as trivial as it is meant to be. And we should be prepared therefore to see his final speech not just as an emotional predicament, but as his ultimate moral tragedy.

Once again Marlowe caps Faustus's great moment with a suggestion of irony, of an impotent fly beating itself to death against a window pane: first the Old Man proves himself immune to the danger from devilish torture which has become a more and more immediate threat to Faustus, and then the Infernal Trinity take up their stations for the catastrophe. Mephostophilis sums up Faustus's position:

> Fond worldling, now his heart-blood dries with grief,
> His conscience kills it, and his labouring brain
> Begets a world of idle fantasies
> To overreach the devil, but all in vain:
> His store of pleasures must be sauced with pain.   V. ii. 12–16

God might have said the same thing. The exultant devils belittle Faustus's attempt to be their master; he cannot overreach them, cannot be as great as Lucifer. The re-entry of Faustus does not immediately re-assert his greatness, but rather detaches us from the struggle of titans for a brief sense of normality, of teacher amongst his students.

When asked why he didn't repent, he states again the simple idea of physical punishment:

> Oft have I thought to have done so; but the devil threatened to tear me in pieces if I named God, to fetch me body and soul if I once gave ear to divinity; and now 'tis too late.   V. ii. 69–72

The complete absence in this prose scene of any profound suggestion, any poetic conception of the issues, of the reality of God and devil, is well-judged: the passions are quieted, the audience lulled before the vast spectacle of eye and ear is built up.

The scholars leave, and Mephostophilis has his last degrading word, hinting that after all it was temptation to which Faustus succumbed:

> 'Twas I, that when thou wert i' the way to heaven,
> Dammed up thy passage; when thou tookst the book
> To view the scriptures, then I turned the leaves
> And led thine eye.   V. ii. 91–4

Faustus remains silent, the Angels pronounce his doom, and introduce the visions of Heaven and Hell that remain with him if not with the audience till the end. Faustus, left alone, is at last fully conscious of his failure, of what he has lost as well as what he has failed to gain. But his predicament is not the simple one of a man in his last hour, knowing his fate: Faustus is not the simple Morality figure caught between Heaven and Hell; his last struggle is still between Heaven, his Hell, and his awareness of his own failure to reach either. When again he turns to Heaven in desperate appeal, he is caught back by the devils who exact the penalty for naming of his Christ:

> See see where Christ's blood streams in the firmament!
> One drop would save my soul, half a drop. Ah my Christ! —
> Rend not my heart for naming of my Christ;   V. ii. 144–6

For the last time Faustus flirts with repentance: but it is something more than flirtation. The vividness of his perception of Christ's propitiatory sacrifice, and the corresponding intimacy of his address, 'Ah my Christ', bring what I have called the other ethos momentarily into full focus.[12] It seems that Faustus is finally able to envisage accepting God's forgiveness, and therefore God's right as well as his power to execute judgment. For the second time in the play, Marlowe entertains an idea of Christianity that might have a meaning, not his usual satiric version. But at either level of experience it is still rejected: Faustus cannot repent because his mind is directed at independence still; or he cannot repent because when he mentions Christ the devils start to tear his heart; and as he offers to repeat his appeal for mercy, torture turns it to Lucifer instead of Christ, and the vision changes:

> Yet will I call on him: oh, spare me Lucifer! —
> Where is it now? 'Tis gone: V. ii. 147–8

[12] I owe this observation to Mr E. A. Horsman.

In the end Faustus does despair, the devil he has constantly feared tears him to pieces, and the scholars draw back the curtain to reveal the gory mess that was 'admirèd man'. But as with *Tamburlaine*, inevitable death does not make a tragedy. *Tamburlaine* is not tragic, *Faustus* is; and the difference lies in Faustus's tortured awareness that it should have been otherwise. Had his Will been what he felt it to be, he would have been triumphant, independent of angels and devils; he would have realized his supreme urge to self-originated power, and Heaven and Hell remained mere fables. But as Faustus fails, greatness as Man imagines it can only remain outside human power, must reside in superhuman God and Devil; and so in the end, it is extinction not mercy that Faustus craves:

> O soul, be changed to little water-drops
> And fall into the ocean, ne'er be found.   V. ii. 183-4

That is not a Christian conclusion; at its tragic end as throughout its length, Marlowe's Morality is inverted; there are still two Hells Lucifer's and Faustus's. But in the end, it would seem Faustus has become fully conscious of Heaven as well. If so, he still cannot or will not accept it: it stands for a way of life he has rejected as unworthy of him; but it happens to be the one God insists upon. Faustus becomes aware, not only that he is wrong, but that the power of God is to have made man desiring a greatness he cannot achieve: that is the constant bitter irony that I have noted throughout the play—man's nature is in direct opposition to his fate. Faustus is the greatest of Marlowe's aspiring heroes in that his consciousness and his achievements are greater than Tamburlaine's; he alone is of fully tragic stature, because only here does Marlowe match his imaginative conception of Man triumphant with a full awareness of Man the feeble and incompetent (in *Edward II* it is Man triumphant that is lacking). He states it both as a bitter and farcical irony, and as a magnificent protest against the creator of this dual nature, his cruel God in whose mouth the word love is the last and greatest mockery.... [We may compare] Marlowe with Blake in his idea of Hell: in the attitude to life adumbrated by the fate of Faustus, he is perhaps nearest to Ibsen, whose heroes' tragic sense also is opposed by an ironic and bitter awareness of futility.

There may seem, then, to be a consistency in Marlowe's attitude to the question of man's place in the universe, the question which forms the dramatic core of *Dr Faustus*. But the attitude is not precisely that of his other plays. Tamburlaine is not obliged to submit to a world order which rejects his aspiration (or at least, not decidedly so). The Jew of Malta and the Guise are: the supporters of order have the last word and therefore, it would seem, Marlowe's approval in their triumph. In neither case, however, is that approval at all certain; he enlarges his exultant Vices beyond the point at which they can just be dismissed with easy approval, but he does not elucidate the implied contradiction. That is what, I think, he sets out to do in *Dr Faustus*, where the ideas of individual freedom or subjection are presented in direct conflict. Faustus, as a Tamburlainish hero, still predominates; but there are already implications that Marlowe doubts his right to do so. There are indications, as Greg points out, that the last scene may have undergone revisions of which we have no clear idea: in the revision Greg suspects, from more formal Morality to the direct tragic speech we know, and certainly in the final removal of the Morality machinery in the 1604 text, there is a reduction of the tragic certainty of the conclusion. The more the Morality trappings are removed, the more Faustus is reduced towards a merely pathetic individual and deprived of the general implication of inevitable moral tragedy the play has suggested. As it stands, there are (as I have said) hints of a submission to a Divine Love that *is* compatible with human dignity. The implication is slight and obscure, and Faustus turns from it to his desire for dissolution. But the ironic emphasis that I have noted on man's inadequacy, and these suggestions of alterations in the last act, with the development of a third term to Faustus's conflict, a credible ethic of Orthodox Christianity, all suggest that if in *Faustus* Marlowe achieved his clearest statement of his ideas, he was already losing confidence in them. *Edward II* does not 'answer' *Dr Faustus;* rather it evades the issue altogether, but its final assertion of political Order has a conviction not apparent in any of Marlowe's earlier work. It echoes a principle accepted without serious question throughout the play; the interest is therefore largely focussed on Edward's individual weakness, his inability to conform to the moral order. It is remarkably well composed, but there is a sense of smallness, of contraction, from Marlowe's earlier work. The stature of *Dr Faustus* is always greater, though its organization is cruder; and the greatness lies in the consistency of Marlowe's attention to a greater matter; to a moral, and not merely an individual, tragedy.

From 'The Moral Tragedy of *Dr Faustus*', in *The Cambridge Journal*, vol. V, no. II, 1952, pp. 662–87 (663–87). The text used in this article is *Dr Faustus: A Conjectural Reconstruction*, W. W. Greg, Clarendon Press, Oxford, 1950.

The Dualism in *Dr Faustus*

... If the Renaissance mind was aflame with thoughts of the splendour of life and of the knowledge and power which were the means to its realization, it was also ... imbued with the knowledge that these flames were the flames of hell and that Faustus would have done better merely to wonder at unlawful things as the Epilogue says, than to be enticed 'To practise magic and concealed arts' (I. i. 103). To see so clearly what eternal joy was and to feel so strongly the desirability of having 'all things that move between the quiet poles ... at my command' (*ibid.*, 57–8), which was its simulacrum, was the tragic dilemma of the Renaissance mind. 'Bi-fold authority!' as Troilus said,

> where reason can revolt
> Without perdition, and loss assume all reason
> Without revolt....

It is within the limits of this dualism that the tragical history of the life and death of Doctor Faustus exists....

What is certainly far from easy but what can at least be pointed to ... are the range and immediacy, the complexity and precision, of the local habitation this dualism has in Marlowe's play. The framework of it may be put in some such simile as that 'the power of scientific knowledge is like the power of black magic.' This tendency to identify the prophecies of astrology with astronomy, the realization of the pagan and sensuous delights of Helen and Cressida with the empirical methods of investigating the natural world, was common enough in the Renaissance world. But if this identification was true for Marlowe, it was also very convenient to his dramatic needs, for it meant that, far from denying the reality of heaven and hell by affirming the reality of the sensuous world, his play could affirm the latter only by affirming the former. The reality of Lucifer, who commands the sensuous world and who is in hell, necessarily implies the reality of Christ and heaven. Mephistophilis himself is forced to bear witness to this, and it is with great subtlety that Marlowe represents Faustus's response to Mephistophilis's damnation. Sometimes, with simple tragic irony, he denies to Mephistophilis's face the reality of damnation: 'Come,' he tells Mephistophilis, 'I think hell's a fable' (II. i. 128). Sometimes he accepts the reality of Mephistophilis's damnation, but with a light-heartedness which is at once appealing and terrifying he says:

This word 'damnation' terrifies me not
For I confound hell in Elysium:
My ghost be with the old philosophers!   I. iii. 61–3

[Quotations are from F. S. Boas's edition, 1932]

And, when Mephistophilis grows 'passionate' at the thought of what he 'that saw the face of God,/And tasted the *eternal* joys of heaven' (*ibid.*, 79–80) must now endure eternally, Faustus urges him with terrifying and fatuous complacency to 'Learn .. of Faustus manly fortitude,/And scorn those joys thou never shalt possess' (*ibid.*, 87–8). For Faustus, too, has put his faith in the application of the empirical method, even to revelation itself. . . . He has put his faith, that is, in man's reason, in those 'thoughts of things divine [which] are inter-mix'd/With scruples and do set the word itself/Against the word,' and has discovered, as he thinks, that, since all men are sinners and the wages of sin damnation, all men must be damned. But he has yet to realize what it means to be damned, and his easy 'fortitude' is to all intents and purposes the equivalent of his 'Come, I think hell's a fable.'

Marlowe's play consists of a series of episodes which exploit this central metaphor of the play, that the power of reason, of scientific thinking, with all that it can do for us and all it will do to us, is the power of black magic. The overt emphasis, in the earlier episodes, is all on what it can do for us, though this overt emphasis is qualified, as the play proceeds, by an increasing emphasis on what it will do to us, by Faustus's increasing awareness of what damnation is. The two attitudes perhaps reach a climax of balance when Faustus cries: 'O, Christ, my Saviour, my Saviour,/Help to save distressed Faustus' soul!' (II. ii. 85–6). And, as the stage direction says, 'Enter Lucifer, Belzebub, and Mephistophilis.' During the early episodes of the play, however, there is an implicit emphasis on the religious attitude which similarly balances the overt emphasis on the rational attitude, that is, the implications of the language and action are always asserting the reality of the authority which Faustus is ignoring or denying. The main resort of the action for this purpose is the continuous presence of the damned Mephistophilis, whose hell is, as he says, always with him. . . .

The main resort of the expression of the play for asserting the reality of divine authority when Faustus is asserting the reality of the senses alone is its steady, ironic application of the religious language, which echoes through the early episodes of the play. 'These metaphysics of magicians,/And necromantic books are *heavenly*' (I. i. 50–1); 'O, this cheers my *soul*' (*ibid.*, 150); 'A sound magician is a *demi-god*' (*ibid.*, 63); 'these books . . . shall make all nations to *canonize* us' (*ibid.*, 120–1); 'The *miracles* that magic will perform' (*ibid.*, 137); and, when Faustus has just finished 'racking the name of God, abjuring the scriptures and his saviour Christ' (I. iii. 49–50) and Mephistophilis has appeared, 'I see there's *virtue* in my *heavenly* words' (*ibid.*, 29); and, when Faustus has signed the bond written in his own blood, '*Consummatum est;* this bill is ended' (II. i. 74). This last case is perhaps the sharpest of them all, that Faustus should have used Christ's last word to signify the completion of his bill; for as Christ's blood had flowed freely that men might be forgiven, so Faustus's had refused to flow that he might write 'Faustus gives to thee his soul' and be enslaved.

Faustus's growing realization of what damnation consists in is almost entirely represented in terms of his understanding of why his blood congealed when he tried to make it flow entirely for sensation, of the limited sense in which necromantic books and Helen are heavenly and time eternal. Perhaps the most impressive of these is his quiet, hopeless, persistent awareness of 'The restless course/That time doth run with calm and silent foot/Shortening my days and thread of vital life' (IV. iiA. 101–3). He does not, of course, to the very end, lose his delight in the sensuous world, though more and more it becomes merely a diversion from the thoughts of damnation—and a diversion more than ever haunted by the ironies of a shadowy Helen and a temporary immortality. Thus it is that in his last great soliloquy Faustus's mind dwells on the evil of those books which put all nature's treasure at his command, the ruin that time has wrought, and the saving grace of Christ's blood. For in order to possess the things of time Faustus has put himself at the mercy of time, and as the terrible clock strikes he can only plead that time may stop in the realm of time itself:

> Stand still, you ever-moving spheres of heaven,
> That time may cease, and midnight never come;
> Fair Nature's eye, rise again, and make
> Perpetual day.. , .
> That Faustus may repent and save his soul!
> O lente, lente currite noctis equi!
> The stars move still, time runs, the clock will strike,
> The devil will come, and Faustus must be damn'd   V. ii. 140–8

For fair nature can do nothing more than she has done for Faustus; and no amount of knowledge about the motion of the ever moving spheres will be enough to give Faustus the power to make them stand still: only prayer can do that, if it can be done at all. It is typical of Marlowe's stressing of the bifold authority of the world of his play, however, that even in this final moment nature should seem fair to Faustus—the very nature the knowledge of whose treasures has damned him—and that Faustus in pleading for time to cease should quote the words of Ovid's lover as he lay in the arms of Corinna. When nature fails him, Faustus turns to Christ; but he cannot reach the saving blood of Christ which he sees streaming through the whole firmament; there is not a drop for him. As a last, hopeless gesture he offers to sacrifice his 'heavenly' necromantic books themselves....

From 'The Tragedy of Marlowe's *Dr Faustus*', in *College English*, vol. V, no. 2, 1943, pp. 70–5 (72–5). The text used in this article is F. S. Boas's edition, Methuen, London, 1932.

WILLIAM EMPSON

Two Proper Crimes

.... Mr Kocher [in his book *Christoper Marlowe*, North Carolina, 1946] writes well about the puzzle of *Faustus*, the question how Marlowe as a declared atheist could feel the story so deeply. He makes clear that Marlowe was fascinated by theology and could write with real horror about the idea of banishment from God. But when Mr Kocher goes on to say that 'there were moments when the ingrained creed sought to take possession of him again, moments when he almost felt that his life had failed of its highest consummation'—in short, that Marlowe was cosily wistful about Christianity, like a Victorian, I feel he misses the whole violence of the thing. If Marlowe had not been murdered so soon he would very probably have been burned alive. It was not hard for him to imagine hell fire. The tension of both realizing and denying the religion was thrust upon him in its most practical form. Surely that is the nerve of the terrific flippancy when Faustus tells Mephistophilis himself that he still doesn't believe in hell. It was not particularly 'cold' of Marlowe, as Mr Kocher thinks, to fail to regard the God of the Christians as a 'tender father.'

In another field Mr Kocher is more optimistic about Marlowe's tenderness. 'The Aristotelian virtue of friendship, on the other hand, was one of his few real enthusiasms within the limits of orthodox principle,' and the friendships of Edward II are given as an example.

This emotion, to a man like Marlowe, 'would be the clearest revelation of human worth, and an intimation, perhaps not of immortality, but of the presence of a spirit of love. . . . It would always be a bond drawing him towards fuller participation in gentler ideals.' The last act of *Edward II* is a crescendo of horror, seen as a punishment deserved by Edward because of his exorbitant love of his favourites. The obscene torture by which he is at last killed is an appalling parody of the homosexual act, and while it is being done the text presumes that the actor will wring the nerves of the audience by his yells: 'I fear me that his cry will rouse the town.'

This does not mean that Marlowe agreed with his audience that the punishment was deserved. Edward gives a long list of classical precedents for his tastes: 'The Roman Tully loved Octavius' and so on; it seems clear that Marlowe felt a good deal of Renaissance snobbery about the matter. The peculiarity of the mind of Marlowe is not that it is 'aspiring' or 'Subjective' or considered 'will invincible' but that it erected absolutely opposed ideals. The unmentionable sin for which the punishment was death was *the proper thing to do*. There are two occasions in the plays when Marlowe piles up the horror in this way, the deaths of Faustus and Edward, and they die because of the two crimes for which Marlowe stood boastfully and defiantly in peril of death. It seems to me that this is the primary fact about his work, and that a critic who muffles it up, from whatever kindly intentions, cannot be saying anything important about him. . . .

From a book review in *The Nation*, vol. CLXIII, 1946, pp. 444–5.

JOHN RUSSELL BROWN

The Quality of Marlowe's Verse

... Marlowe did not pursue comparisons so nimbly [as Kyd and the early Shakespeare] and seldom developed an intricate argument; he preferred to build, to progress by marked degrees, retaining each element within the final large impression. Tamburlaine, Gaveston, Edward, Faustus, Barabas are all presented this way. Barabas can tell his life-story phase by phase, to give a definite, forceful impression (II, iii, 177–95). He argues by independent statements and questions; in the following speech the steps of his deliberations are marked by alternate roman and italic type:

> My gold, my gold, and all my wealth is gone.
> *You partial heavens, have I deserved this plague?*
> What, will you thus oppose me, luckless stars,
> To make me desperate in my poverty?
> *And knowing me impatient in distress*
> *Think me so mad as I will hang myself*
> That I may vanish o'er the earth in air,
> And leave no memory that e're I was.
> *No, I will live; nor loathe I this my life:*
> *And since you leave me in the ocean thus*
> *To sink or swim, and put me to my shifts,*
> *I'll rouse my senses, and awake myself.*
> Daughter, I have it: *thou perceiv'st the plight*
> *Wherein these Christians have oppressèd me:*
> Be ruled by me, for in extremity
> We ought to make bar of no policy.   I. ii. 258–73

In this passage the progress of his thought is clear, but only a recognition of the distinctive characteristics of the successive elements of Marlowe's rhetoric will reveal the varied and rich responses that are drawn together, and hence the speech's ability to give an impression of a lively, self-contained mind. This kind of elaboration is as minutely controlled as Kyd's or Shakespeare's; perhaps more so, for it is not at the mercy of a repeated rhetorical pattern. Tamburlaine's address when Zenocrate is shown on her death-bed (2*T*, II, iv) has something of a rhetorician's parallelism; but its units are large and firmly marked by the refrain, so that the first dark and angry impressions are held together with the concluding revelation of Tamburlaine's harmony of soul as he considers his own death with his queen's. The careful, large-spanned verbal architecture is perhaps most noticeable when several characters speak in chorus to establish a situation and display its diverse aspects, as they do in the opening of the last scene of *Tamburlaine*. But while the structure is not always obvious on the surface of the dialogue, it is basic; and it must be understood—like an argument or diagram—and given emphasis by varying verbal techniques and physical embodiments, if an actor wishes to render the full interest of Marlowe's poetry. . . .

Even passages that sound at first like bombast can reveal a kind of precision. . . . Through all the great and thundering words, the actor must search for an intellectual energy and control. Here is the main difference from Shakespeare, in whose plays we look always for verbal and metrical expressiveness, for implicit meaning and feeling. Behind the rhetorical design of Shakespeare's earliest dialogue and behind the rhetoric's more subtle manipulation in later work, we have learned how to find psychological realism, a representation of the inner workings of thought and emotion. This is conveyed by tone, choice of words, linked associations, fleeting transitions of subject or mood, syntactical variety, the pulse and irregularities of the metre. It is this continual expressiveness that Marlowe lacks: when a stage-direction says '*The king rageth*', the verse-lines and syntactical units continue to work easily together; the vocabulary is not simplified or changed in other ways:

> I'll not resign, but whilst I live—
> Traitors, be gone, and join you with Mortimer!
> Elect, conspire, install, do what you will;
> Their blood and yours shall seal these treacheries.   *E2*, V, i. 86-9

The varied content, the weight or force of each separate utterance within the speech, represents feeling as well as cumulative meaning; but there is hardly any realistic impression of enraged utterance. When Marlowe resorted to prose for Zabina's grief (*1T*, V, ii.) he introduced a much more elaborate system of rhetorical repetition to give distinct phases to her distraction. When he shows Tamburaline in the last agonies of his sickness, the verse-lines remain full and regular; the architecture of his dialogue is still firm; there is comparison and allusion: indeed precision and compounded effect are notable characteristics even in the death-struggle. . . .

From 'Marlowe and the Actors', *Tulane Drama Review*, vol. 8, no. 4, Summer 1964, pp. 155-73 (157-62).

C. S. LEWIS

Hero and Leander

.... When we speak of 'innocence' in connexion with the first two sestiads we are using the word 'innocence' in a very peculiar sense. We mean not the absence of guilt but the absence of sophistication, the splendour, though a guilty splendour, of unshattered illusions. Marlowe's part of the poem is the most shameless celebration of sensuality which we can find in English literature. ...

In reading [Shakespeare's] *Venus and Adonis* we see lust: in reading Marlowe's sestiads we see not lust but what lust thinks it sees. We do not look at the passion itself: we look out from it upon a world transformed by the hard, brittle splendour of erotic vision. Hence all the sickly weight and warmth which makes unrestrained appetite in the real world so unpleasant to the spectator or even, perhaps, in retrospect to the principals themselves, does not appear at all. Instead of Shakespeare's sweating palms and poutings and pantings and duckings and 'lustful language broken' and 'impatience' that 'chokes the pleading tongue' we have a gigantic insolence of hyperbole. The real world, which Shakespeare cannot quite forget, is by Marlowe smashed into bits, and he makes glory out of the ruin. Hero has been offered Apollo's throne. The brightness of her neck makes a collar of pebbles shine like diamonds by reflection. The sun will not burn her hands. The ladies of Sestos, walking in procession, make the street a 'firmament of breathing stars'. In that world there are boys so beautiful that they can never drink in safety from a fountain: the water nymphs would pull them in.

If you compare these hyperboles with one of Shakespeare's you will easily see the difference. His Venus promises Adonis that her hand will 'dissolve or seem to melt' in his. That, of course, is hyperbolical, but it is in touch with fact—with the fact that hands may be hot, moist, and soft. But Marlowe's hyperboles are so towering that they become mythopoeic. They have, none the less, their own wild consistency and co-operate in building up such a world as passion momentarily creates, a topsy-turvy world where beauty is omnipotent and the very laws of nature are her willing captives. This mythopoeic quality is reinforced by Marlowe's use of what may be called the aetiological conceit, as in his passage about Mercury and the fates at the end of I, or his explanation why 'since *Heroes* time hath halfe the world been blacke'. Though the whole two sestiads celebrate the flesh, flesh itself, undisguised, rarely appears in them for long. Leander's beauty is presented half mythically: he is a prize like the golden fleece, his body is as 'straight as Circe's wand', and the description of him shines with the names of *Nectar, Pelops, Jove*, and the cold *Cinthia*.

With this style there go two other characteristics. One, of course, is the metre—a ringing and often end-stopped couplet, compared with which the stanza of *Venus and Adonis* is unprogressive and the enjambed couplets of *Endymion* invertebrate. I suspect that the masculine quality of the verse, in fruitful tension with the luxury of the matter, plays an important part in making so much pure honey acceptable: it is a beautiful example of Wordsworth's theory of metre. The other is the total absence of tenderness. You must not look in Marlowe for what Dryden called 'the softnesses of love'. You must, indeed, look for love itself only in the narrowest sense. Love here is not 'ful of pittie' but 'deaffe and cruell': his temple is a blaze of grotesques. Leander woos like 'a bold sharpe sophister'. The male and immortal lover who first tries to ravish him, ends by trying to kill him. Hero is compared to diamonds, and the whole work has something of their hardness and brightness. Marlowe sings a love utterly separated from kindness, *cameraderie*, or friendship. . . . But, however shocking, this treatment is an artistic success. We know from some terrible scenes in Keats's *Endymion* how dangerous it is to attempt the mixture of tenderness and sensuality in verse. Licentious poetry, if it is to remain endurable, must generally be heartless: as it is in Ovid, in Byron, in Marlowe himself. If it attempts pathos or sweetness an abyss opens at the poet's feet. Marlowe never comes near that abyss. His poem, though far from morally pure, has purity of another sort—purity of form and colour and intention. We may feel, as we come to the end of the Second Sestiad, that we have been mad, but we do not feel that we have been choked or contaminated. And yet I believe that the final impression left on an adult's mind is not one of madness or even of splendour, but, oddly enough, of pathos. If we had caught Marlowe striving after that effect in such a poem we should perhaps have turned from him with contempt. But it is not so. What moves us is simply our knowledge that this passionate splendour, so insolent, so defiant, and so 'unconscious of mortality', is 'desperately mortal'.

That it was doomed, for Hero and Leander, to end in misery Marlowe of course knew well. He wrote only the first movement of the story, the ascending movement; how he would have handled the descent we do not know. . . .

From '*Hero and Leander*' by C. S. Lewis, in *Proceedings of the British Academy*, vol. XXXVIII, Oxford University Press, London, 1952, pp. 23–37 (23–7).

Select Bibliography

The works of Christopher Marlowe

Collected Editions

Marlowe's *Works* were edited by G. Robinson, 3 vols., London, 1826; by Alexander Dyce, 3 vols., London, 1850; by F. Cunningham, London, 1870; and by A. H. Bullen, 3 vols., London, 1885. The *Plays* were edited for the Mermaid Series by H. Havelock Ellis, London, 1887, new ed. 1951. The standard one volume edition of the *Works* was edited by C. F. Tucker Brooke, Oxford, 1910. The standard six-volume edition, General Editor R. H. Case, Staten Island, N.Y., Gordian Press, 1930–33, is made up as follows: *The Life of Marlowe* and *Dido*, ed. C. F. T. Brooke, 1930; *Tamburlaine the Great*, ed. U. M. Ellis-Fermor, 1930, 2nd ed. 1951; *The Jew of Malta* and *The Massacre at Paris*, ed. H. S. Bennett, 1931; *Dr Faustus*, ed. F. S. Boas, 1932, 2nd ed. 1949; *Edward II*, ed. H. B. Charlton and R. D. Waller, 1933, 2nd ed. rev. by F. N. Lees, 1955; *Poems*, ed. L. C. Martin, 1931. The *Plays* were edited by L. Kirschbaum, Cleveland, Ohio, 1962. There is an *Everyman* edition of the *Plays and Poems*, no. 383, London, repr. 1963; and a *World's Classics* edition of the *Plays*, no 578, London, 1939, repr. 1966.

Recent Editions of Separate Plays

The Jew of Malta, ed. R. van Fossen, London, 1964, is in Regents Renaissance Drama Series; *Dr Faustus*, ed. Roma Gill, 1965, *The Jew of Malta*, ed. T. W. Craik, 1966, and *Edward II*, ed. W. M. Merchant, 1968, all London, are in New Mermaids Series; *Dr Faustus*, ed. J. D. Jump, London 1962, is in the Revels Plays Series; *Dido, Queen of Carthage*, and *The Massacre at Paris*, ed. H. J. Oliver, London, 1968; *Dr Faustus*, ed. J. D. Jump, 1965, and *Tamburlaine*, ed. Tatiana Wolff, 1964, both London, are in Methuens English Classics; *Edward II*, ed. Roma Gill, London, 1967, is an Oxford University Press publication.

Biographical and Critical Studies

Books

John Bakeless, *Christopher Marlowe, the Man in His Time*, New York, Washington Square Press; *The Tragicall History of Christopher Marlowe*, Hamden, Conn., Shoe String Press, 1942.

R. W. Battenhouse, *Marlowe's Tamburlaine: A Study in Renaissance Moral Philosophy*, Nashville, Tenn., Vanderbilt Univ. Press, 1964.

David M. Bevington, *From Mankind to Marlowe*, Cambridge, Mass., Harvard Univ. Press, 1962.

Frederick S. Boas, *Christopher Marlowe*, Oxford Univ. Press, 1940; *Marlowe and His Circle*, New York, Russell & Russell, 1968.

Muriel C. Bradbrook, *Themes and Conventions of Elizabethan Tragedy*, Cambridge Univ. Press, 1952–60, Chap. 6; *The School of Night*, Cambridge Univ. Press, 1936, pp. 101–24.

John P. Brockbank, *Doctor Faustus by Marlowe*, Woodbury, N.Y., Barron's Educational Series, 1962.

Douglas Cole, *Suffering and Evil in the Plays of Christopher Marlowe*, Princeton, N.J., Princeton Univ. Press, 1962.

Mark Eccles, *Christopher Marlowe in London*, New York, Octagon Press, 1967.

U. M. Ellis-Fermor, *Christopher Marlowe*, Hamden, Conn., Shoe String Press.

Philip Henderson, *Christopher Marlowe*, London, Writers and Their Work Series, 1956, rev. ed., 1966.

Leslie Hotson, *The Death of Christopher Marlowe*, New York, Russell & Russell, 1925.

Paul Kocher, *Christopher Marlowe: A Study of His Thought, Learning, and Character*, New York, Russell & Russell, 1946.

G. Wilson Knight, *The Golden Labyrinth: A Study of English Drama*, New York, W. W. Norton, Inc., 1962.

Harry Levin, *The Overreacher: A Study of Christopher Marlowe*, Boston, Beacon Press, 1964.

Michel Poirier, *Christopher Marlowe*, Hamden, Conn., Shoe String Press, 1968.

Wilbur Sanders, *The Dramatist and the Received Idea*, Cambridge Univ. Press, 1968.

J. B. Steane, *Marlowe: A Critical Study*, Cambridge Univ. Press, 1964.

Frank P. Wilson, *Marlowe and the Early Shakespeare*, Oxford Univ. Press, 1953.

A. D. Wraight, *In Search of Christopher Marlowe: A Pictorial Biography*, New York, Vanguard Press, 1965. (Excellent pictures but a poor text.)

Essays and Articles

General:

C. F. T. Brooke, 'Marlowe', in *Essays on Shakespeare and Other Elizabethans*, New Haven, 1948, pp. 179–97; 'The Reputation of Christopher Marlowe', *Transactions of Connecticut Academy of Arts and Sciences*, vol. 25, 1922, pp. 347–408.

John Russell Brown, 'Marlowe and the Actors', *Tulane Drama Review*, [*TDR*], vol. 8, no. 4, 1964, pp. 155–73. This issue is devoted entirely to Marlowe.

T. S. Eliot, 'Christopher Marlowe', in *Selected Essays*, London, 1932, 3rd ed. 1951, pp. 118–25.

William Empson, 'Two Proper Crimes', *The Nation*, vol. CLXIII, 1946, pp. 444–5.

L. C. Knights, 'The Strange Case of Christopher Marlowe', in *Further Explorations*, London, 1965, pp. 75–98.

M. M. Mahood, 'Marlowe's Heroes', in *Poetry and Humanism*, London, 1950, pp. 54–86.

J. C. Maxwell, 'Christopher Marlowe', in *The Age of Shakespeare*, ed. Boris Ford, London, 1955, pp. 162–78.

Mario Praz, 'Christopher Marlowe', *English Studies*, vol. 13, 1931, pp. 209–23.

I. Ribner, 'Marlowe and the Critics', *TDR*, vol. 8, no. 4, 1964, pp. 211–24.

Ethel Seaton, 'Marlowe's Light Reading', in *Elizabethan and Jacobean Studies, presented to F. P. Wilson, in Honour of his 70th Birthday*, Oxford, 1959, pp. 17–35.

William Urry, 'Marlowe and Canterbury', *Times Literary Supplement*, Feb. 13, 1964, p. 136.

On *Tamburlaine*

G. I. Duthie, 'The Dramatic Structure of *Tamburlaine the Great*, Parts I and II', *English Studies (Essays and Studies*, N.S. vol I), 1948 pp. 101–26.

Helen Gardner, 'The Second Part of *Tamburlaine the Great*', *Modern Language Review [MLR]*, vol. XXXVII, 1942, pp. 18–24.

I. Ribner, 'The Idea of History in Marlowe's *Tamburlaine*', *Journal of English Literary History [ELH]*, vol. XX, 1953, pp. 251–66.

Ethel Seaton, 'Marlowe's Map', *Essays and Studies*, vol. X, 1924, pp. 13–35.

On *The Jew of Malta*

Antonio D'Andrea, 'Marlowe's Prologue to *The Jew of Malta*', *Mediaeval and Renaissance Studies*, vol. V, 1961, pp. 214–48.

Howard B. Babb, '*Policy* in Marlowe's *Jew of Malta*', *ELH*, vol. XXIV, 1957, pp. 85–94.

Leo Kirschbaum, 'Some Light on *The Jew of Malta*', *Modern Langugae Quarterly [MLQ]*, vol. VII, 1946, pp. 53–6.

On *Edward II*

L. J. Mills, 'The Meaning of *Edward II*', *Modern Philology*, vol. XXXII, 1934, pp. 11–31.

Clifford Leech, 'Marlowe's *Edward II*: Power and Suffering', *Critical Quarterly [CQ]*, vol. I, no. 3, 1959, pp. 181–96.

On *Dr Faustus*

Nicholas Brooke, 'The Moral Tragedy of *Dr Faustus*', *Cambridge Journal*, vol. V, no. 11, 1952, pp. 662–87.

Lily B. Campbell, '*Dr Faustus:* A Case of Conscience', *Publications of the Modern Language Association of America* [*PMLA*], vol. LXII, 1952, pp. 219–39.

Jerzy Grotowski, '*Dr Faustus* in Poland', *TDR*, vol. 8, no. 4, 1964, pp. 120–33.

W. W. Greg, 'The Damnation of Faust', *MLR*, vol. XLI, 1946, pp. 97–107.

Erich Heller, 'Faust's Damnation: The Morality of Knowledge', *Listener*, Jan. 11, 1962, pp. 59–61.

Harold Jenkins, Review of Greg's *Faustus*, *MLR*, vol. XLVI, 1951, pp. 82–6.

P. H. Kocher, 'Nashe's Authorship of the Prose Scenes in *Faustus*', *MLQ*, vol. III, 1942, pp. 17–40.

Leo Kirschbaum, 'Marlowe's *Faustus:* A Reconsideration', *Review of English Studies*, vol. XIX, 1943, pp. 225–41.

T. McAlinden, 'Classical Mythology and Christian Tradition in Marlowe's *Dr Faustus*', *PMLA*, vol. LXXXI, 1966, pp. 214–23.

Arthur Mizener, 'The Tragedy of Marlowe's *Dr Faustus*', *College English*, vol. V, no. 2, 1943, pp. 72–5.

D. J. Palmer, 'Magic and Poetry in *Dr Faustus*', *CQ*, vol. 6, no. 1, 1964, pp. 56–67.

James Smith, 'Marlowe's *Dr Faustus*', *Scrutiny*, vol. VIII, no. 1, 1939, pp. 36–55.

On *Hero and Leander*

M. C. Bradbrook, '*Hero and Leander*', *Scrutiny*, vol. II, no. 1, 1933, pp. 59–64.

C. S. Lewis, '*Hero and Leander*', *Proceedings of the British Academy*, vol. XXXVIII, 1952, pp. 23–37.